BERLIN AIRLIFT

11/4/03

To
Bess Vaughan Etter

with

Best Regards!

[signature]

 Joseph Werner

Among other things...
Creator of the term "Silent Majority"

7 High Gate Drive
Setauket, NY 11733 (USA)
631-751-8170 • FAX 631-751-8170
e-mail: allright@optonline.net
Website: www.josephwerner.com

BERLIN AIRLIFT:

BRIDES and GROOMS CREATED

By
Joseph Werner

Water Edge Publishing Co.
Box 1132, Main Street
Stony Brook, New York 11790
631 (~~516~~) 751-8170

Gail S. Halvorsen Col USAF Ret.

September 26, 1997

To whom it may concern:

SUBJECT: ABOUT THE AUTHOR

I have known Joseph (Joe) Werner for about 11 years. Seldom have I found a more dedicated champion of individual rights in the local, national, or international arenas. For his efforts I have nick named him, "The International Freedom Fighter".

Joe has been a voice for those who feel they lack a voice, such as those we class as the silent majority. He is 100% committed to those whose cause he believes is just and it is not just a token representation. Many times Joe has invested his own resources for the benefit of others. Only one example is what he did for those behind the infamous Berlin Wall. In their behalf he maintained a candlelight vigil every August 13th for 10 years at his own expense until the "Wall" came down.

The book is a factual account of the valiant Berliners before and after the time of the Berlin Airlift. That would be enough but in addition the book is capped off by his extensive research into the story of the lives and the subsequent human dynamics between some American men who were involved in the Berlin Airlift and the delightful German women who were to become their wives. The story is unique and captivating.

This personal human story is both enlightening and entertaining. I highly recommend it!

Sincerely,

Gail S. Halvorsen
Gail S. Halvorsen
Col. USAF Ret.
"The Berlin Candy Bomber"

Copyright © 1998 by
JOSEPH WERNER

Library of Congress
Catalog Card Number: 98-061448

ISBN: 0-9666846-0-5

Water Edge Publishing Co.
Box 1132, Main Street
Stony Brook, New York 11790
Tel/Fax (~~516~~ 631) 751-8170
E mail: allright@~~villagenet.com~~ optonline.net

cover, layout, photo retouching
by: Desktop Publishing Plus

ALL RIGHTS RESERVED
PRIOR PERMISSION REQUIRED FOR
REPRODUCTION IN ANY FORM.

Printed in the United States of America

PINE HILL PRESS, INC.
Freeman, S. Dak. 57029

BERLIN AIRLIFT
PEACE WARRIORS' ETERNAL ECHO

Engines roar in the Berlin sky from planes that aren't there,
    It's the eternal echo of the Airlift that proved the free world cared.
Roads were blocked to West Berlin and trains to there held still,
    Starvation, cold and outright despair with freedom its intent to kill.
Mothers sighed, children cried, and fathers didn't know what to do,
    World War II just ended and the blockade came out of the blue.
Would the free world countries help them or would they fade away,
    Was the thought of West Berliners as the hours ticked away.
Their question was soon answered by America's General Clay,
    He ordered the Berlin Airlift to begin without delay!
Millions of Berliners for a year and more were flown survival needs,
    Planes flew tight through day and night—an "Air Bridge"
        to accomplish the deed.
They were flown by daring PEACE WARRIORS who knew their
    life could end,
    But the PEACE WARRIORS were willing to take the risk—to help
    their new found friends.
The blockade finally ended with West Berliners' freedom in tact,
    Thanks to many determined Germans, English, French
        and America's Might MAT.*

—Joseph Werner

---

*Military Air Transport

Contents

Introduction

1. Through Tragedy Came Love 7

2. Anna Maria & Severino DiCocco 23

3. Eva & Paul Hawkins 57

4. Annie & Bill Michaels 83

5. Ellie & James Spatafora 111

6. Hedda & Forrest Ott 137

7. Loves That Have Lasted 159

Acknowledgements

Introduction

I had no idea when I saw the Berlin Wall for the first time in 1978 I would be so affected by its horror that three years later August 13, 1981, the 20th anniversary of the building of the wall, I would launch a one-man ten-year, self-financed catalytic "international" Berlin Wall Demise Campaign at Checkpoint Charlie entrance to the Berlin Wall. My campaign became so effective the Stasi (secret East German police) had me under surveillance.

Though the vigils held "every" August 13th until the wall came down, plus an all-night Christmas vigil in 1988, totaled approximately 200 hours, they were only one aspect of my "international" campaign. Other aspects included: designating the Black Flag as an international "Symbol of Sorrow" for Germans held behind the Berlin Wall and giving 1,000 small black flags to visitors to my vigils; writing of the "Berlin Wall Trilogy" (phases of wall crossing from the East); "Share the Sorrow for a Day" in which I asked Berlins in America to act as though there was a Berlin Wall in their Berlin (Berlin, Pennsylvania made me an honorary citizen); "World Project to End World's Shame" in which more than fifty world leaders were sent letters with my hand-drawn map of a section in a major city in their country showing and naming streets where an imaginary Berlin Wall type might exist. Leaders were requested to do what they could to help have the Berlin Wall taken down in a peaceful manner. There were many, many, many more aspects to my campaign!

Through the years my Berlin Wall Demise Campaign received coverage from most if not all major news services of the world including the Associated Press, United Press, Reuters and German Press Association (dpa), etc.

As time went by during my campaign for the wall's demise, I became more and more aware of the Berlin Airlift and its importance to Germany and the rest of the Free World. The seed into this area was planted during my 1985 vigil at Checkpoint Charlie entrance to the Berlin Wall when a German lady having read a story in a prestigious Berlin newspaper of my contacting Berlins in America requesting they "Share the Sorrow for a Day." The lady gave me rare limited edition Memorial Plates of the "35th Anniversary of the Ending of the Berlin Airlift." Through an interpreter, she told me she had been a hungry child during the Berlin blockade and received food because of the Berlin Airlift. She then said she knew that what I would do with the Memorial Plates would be something good! I established the "Johanna Hoppe Award" to be given to an individual, organization or government that had done something very outstanding for Berlin and/or Berliners, I selected and gave the award to each of the following:

<u>Berlin, Connecticut</u> – Participated in "Share the Sorrow for a Day"

<u>Berlin, New Hampshire </u>– Participated in "Share the Sorrow for a Day"

<u>Berlin, Pennsylvania</u> – Participated in "Share the Sorrow for a Day"

<u>Berlin Airlift Veterans Association (BAVA)</u> – Participants in the Berlin Airlift

Introduction (3)

Gail Halvorsen (Col. USAF Ret.) – "The Berlin Candy Bomber" Berlin Airlift pilot who dropped little parachutes laden with candy and gum for the Berlin children.

Berlin Airlift Historical Foundation (BAHF) – Found, purchased and then made a C-54, type plane used in the Berlin Airlift, into a flying museum and classroom of the Berlin Airlift era.

Mr. and Mrs. Gunther Jansen – Translated news releases and correspondence to and from German.

General Lucius D. Clay (Posthumously) – American Military Governor of the US Zone of Occupation in Germany ordered the Berlin Airlift to begin when the Soviet Union blockaded land routes to West Berlin.

General William H. Tunner (Posthumously) – Commanding General of the Combined Air Lift Task Force. It is doubtful the Berlin Airlift could have succeeded without his expertise and leadership. He was the world's foremost authority of large air cargo transportation.

In time I wrote a tribute to participants in the Berlin Airlift entitled, BERLIN AIRLIFT (Peace Warriors' Eternal Echo), and in 1992 was invited to San Antonio, Texas as a guest of the Berlin Airlift Veterans Association (BAVA) at its annual reunion where I was made an honorary-life member. In addition to speaking before BAVA members in San Antonio, Texas, I also spoke at the 1994 reunion in Berlin, Germany, 1996 reunion in Dayton, Ohio and the 1997 reunion in Colorado Springs, Colorado.

I had been aware some members of the American military who participated in the Berlin Airlift had married German ladies but the thought of writing a book about it didn't occur to me until 1996 while watching the happiness permeated throughout the room at the Welcome Reception for the Berlin Airlift Veterans Association Reunion being held in Dayton, Ohio. Research for the book began at this reunion.

The book is a historical and factual account of five German ladies who became the brides of five American military men (grooms) who were participants in the Berlin Airlift. Each bride and groom was given an all-encompassing questionnaire to answer, specifically worded for their gender. A lot of latitude was given each bride and groom to express their innermost thoughts and feelings. Questions ranged from: date of birth; family structure; youth; attitude before, during and after World War II and the Berlin Airlift; how they met their spouse; problems in courtship and/or obtaining a marriage license, emigration to the United States; the reaction of relatives and friends in both countries; how many children (and grandchildren), if any, do they now have and many other interesting and informative questions. (A broad leeway was given to add any information they felt pertinent.) The concluding question asks, "Why are you so proud and happy that the love of your life became your wife/husband?"

A separate chapter is devoted to each couple with the questions and answers quoted verbatim.

The book is structured to present readers with five separate love stories, love stories that developed during a period of extreme hardship and tension. It is unique! It is history as it happened told by people who were

Introduction (5)

there, hidden things you don't ordinarily find in books. It includes personal stories rarely told except to close friends or in discussion with individuals who had been in similar situations during World War II and the blockade of Berlin.

The first chapter in the book gives a background of the devastation in Berlin at the end of World War II and events leading up to the Soviet's Berlin blockade which in turn brought other former German war adversaries to work with Berliners and other Germans as a team in the world's greatest military humanitarian operations—"The Berlin Airlift!" In a phrase heard often in Germany when speaking of the Berlin Airlift, "They came as Conquerors and left as Friends!"

The final chapter is one of praise and tells of a common thread of strength, love and determination this author uncovered that each bride and groom possess. Even they as individuals never realized they possess the aforementioned in common as there had never been a reason for analysis or comparison.

Family trees that developed combined with several other factors noted are discussed in detail to illustrate the success of their marriages. Their success has been of benefit to their children, their children's children, their friends and relatives and their countries of origin. These "Berlin Airlift: Brides and Grooms Created" certainly have a reason to be proud! This is a rare book that has no boundaries for potential readership!

CHAPTER 1

Through Tragedy Came Love

Though my first visit to Berlin, Germany in 1978 had occurred some 33 years after World War II ended, war type tension was immediately obvious upon leaving the luggage area at Tegel Airport after a flight from Frankfurt, Germany. I had just been to three countries, Austria, England, and France with the standard passport check when entering each country.

Upon picking up my luggage I proceeded to go into the main terminal on my way to the Kempinski Hotel where I had lodging reservations. Although the flight originated in Frankfurt, Germany and this was Berlin, Germany, all passengers had to stop to be questioned by a man in uniform behind what appeared to be bullet proof glass. This was highly unusual as nowhere else did one have to undergo such a process that normally only occurs during one's first entrance into the country. It was an uncomfortable feeling to be questioned by this man who didn't smile and looked very stern. The wall behind him was filled with photographs of the type of people one would see on any US Post Office WANTED poster. Police with automatic military guns were seen throughout the airport and looked as though they were highly trained to use them.

As mentioned in the Introductory Chapter, it was during this first visit that I saw the Berlin Wall and vowed to do all I could to help have the Wall taken down in a peaceful manner.

I wasn't in Berlin just before or just after World War II ended to see the devastation that had taken place with bodies and body parts seen everywhere, with buildings in complete ruin as described by the German soldier Siegfried Knappe in his book "Soldat." Nor was I there to see the near starvation and subhuman living conditions Germans had to undergo—I will however tell what others who were there told me.

The things I did see when in Berlin for my vigils, which occurred at least once every year from 1981 until the Wall came down, gave me strong indications of the horrible living conditions thrust upon Germans at the end of World War II; and to some Berliners, the added horror of living under the Soviet Union's cruel control behind the Berlin Wall.

I saw the Anhalter Bahnhof that was once one of Germany's busiest train stations completely leveled to the ground with only a sheet of pieces of cement and stone rising up from the ground. The sheet *itself* left standing looked like a skeleton with 60% of its parts missing. This illustrates the misery, death and hardship that must have occurred.

The Kaiser Wilhelm Church located on the Kurfürstendum, the "Fifth Avenue of Berlin," has been kept in the condition it had been when World War II ended. It now stands as a Memorial and reminder of the war's destructive power. Only a small scarred section reaching for the sky is left of this once tremendously strong church built of large blocks of stone. The sadness of what the war had done is made even more obvious when one sees the Kaiser Whilhelm Church Memorial surrounded by all new and modern buildings that has been brought about by the luxury of peace and freedom. Many, many similar sights were seen throughout Berlin during my visits. One had only to take a bus ride through the streets of Berlin to see where bombs and bullets left their mark of war's bitter destruction. Berlin no doubt represented similar destruction that existed in many other areas of Germany.

How miserable it must have been for Germans. Where did they live? How did they get food? How did they survive? These thoughts with the knowledge obtained by the sights during my many visits to Berlin made me aware of the utter destruction that had taken place and the hardship Germans had undergone when the war ended. Because of this I hold the Brides in this book in the *highest* regard. They survived the stress of war and the losses incurred in its aftermath as did many Americans who survived the Great Depression. Both underwent excruciating pain and became stronger in the process of overcoming it.

As you read this book you will find the Germans had great fear of the advancing Russian soldiers. It is difficult for people from the free world to envision the extent of harshness and cruelty the Soviet Union was capable of under Stalin. The *200* or so hours of vigils I spent at the Checkpoint Charlie entrance to the Berlin Wall as one of the segments of my *ten-year international campaign* to do everything I could to help have the Berlin Wall taken down in a peaceful manner taught me a lot about Russian cruelty and why Germans had reason to fear them.

On one occasion during one of my vigils at Checkpoint Charlie, a lady walked across the dividing line to an East German policeman standing in the middle of the road on the East side. She gave the East German policeman a bouquet of flowers and asked that he give the bouquet and her regards to her relative who was in the East. The next day I was told the lady's relative in the East was put in prison because of the publicity the lady had given him.

As part of my international Berlin Wall Demise Campaign I had designated the Black Flag as an international SYMBOL of SORROW for Germans held behind the Berlin Wall. In 1983 I began giving 1000 small black flags to visitors at each of my vigils. During a lull period in the latter part of the day of one vigil I was in conversation with a Berliner who spoke English. Suddenly a rather slender man probably in his 50's raised one of the Black Flags up in the air and as though he was a cavalry officer with a sword in his hand giving orders to "Charge!" went into the East Berlin sector yelling and waving the flag high until we lost sight of him when he made a turn to go into the East border checkpoint.

After a short time, the man came running toward the West in an awkward and uncoordinated manner as though in a state of fear.

At the same time an East German guard was running in the street parallel to him toward the West until the guard got to the end of a cyclone fence that went about two-thirds of the way toward the West. This fence separated the sidewalk from the street. There was another cyclone fence that went further toward the West and was on the left side of the sidewalk where the man was now running toward the West. When the guard got past the fence that separated the two, he rushed to the man grabbed him and harshly banged him several times against the fence that had been on the man's left side, and then in a very rough and abrupt manner, pushed the man toward the direction of West Berlin. As I wanted the MP's to know I had no part in the incident, I went to the American MP's there at Checkpoint Charlie and told them we were caught by complete surprise when the man went to the East as he did. The MP told me not to worry about it that the Russians emptied their prisons and mental institutions and sent the people from them to the West. Some of those people hate the East and do such things as the man had done. (When I had time to reflect and give further thought to what happened, I realized Castro had done the same thing with people in prisons and mental institutions in Cuba and sent them to the United States.)

To most of the world, World War II was ancient history in 1981; to Germans living in East Berlin it was an everyday reality. The Berlin Wall that the Russians built in essence kept Germans as "prisoners of war" in their own country, 40 or so years after the war had ended. If the Soviet Union was doing this to Berliners at this time (1981), imagine what they must have done when they entered Berlin as victors in World War II. One lady from a small town in Germany told me during one of the two post graduate courses I had taken on German and Austrian history in 1978 that there wasn't a single female in her small town who hadn't been raped by a Russian soldier.

Because my attention to the horrors of the Berlin Wall was so intense, I hadn't given thought to the fact that it was here in West Berlin that the Berlin Airlift—the world's greatest humanitarian operation ever undertaken by the military—had occurred. Almost as soon as I was reminded of this fact—while holding one of my annual August 13th vigils in 1985 at Checkpoint Charlie—I began realizing that I with all other West Berliners on this day (as during the Berlin blockade) was actually on an "Island of Freedom." West Berlin was completely surrounded by Soviet Union military forces.

The United States, United Kingdom, France and the Soviet Union who, less than five years before the Berlin blockade had been Allies in World War II against Germany, were now divided in post war occupation. The attempt by the Soviet Union to drive its former Allies out of Berlin with the blockade caused General Lucius D. Clay, the US Deputy Military Governor to Germany, to order the Berlin Airlift which flew over the Soviet Zone from free Germany to free West Berlin.

Americans, British and French worked as a team with Germans to provide food, coal and other survival needs via this "Air Bridge" to more than 2.5 million West Berliners. James Spatafora, then a 19-year-old US Air Force member (one of the "grooms" featured in this book) stated, "Seven times more tonnage of survival needs for Berliners was flown into West Berlin during the Berlin Airlift than the total tonnage in bombs dropped on Berlin during all of World War II." In the minds of Berliners, the status of these victors of the war changed from an "Occupation Army" to "Protectors." In the minds of most Germans today, we are the best of friends.

It is important to know the background of torment the "German Brides" in this book went through and the compassion felt by their "American Grooms" to the suffering the Soviet Union's Berlin blockade had thrust upon them. Their love stories are the main subject of this book and this author is attempting to briefly inform you of important facts of the Berlin Airlift so you can better appreciate the rock solid marriages that the Airlift produced.

Some of the major highlight events that have a bearing on the Berlin Airlift are listed in chronological order plus brief summaries of other important facts follow: *(Information obtained from several sources* including Henrick Bering's "Outpost Berlin" and the Berlin Airlift Gratitude Foundation's "Blockade and Airlift: Legend or Lesson?"

(1) <u>May 8, 1945</u>: Germany unconditionally surrendered thus ending World War II.

(2) <u>June 23, 1948</u>: Soviet Union cut off electricity to Berlin from large power plant in its zone. Local West Berlin electrical plants were unable to make up the loss thus Berlin left in veritable darkness.

(3) <u>June 24, 1948</u>: Roads, trains and water traffic were shut down by the Soviet Union—making the Berlin blockade complete.

(4) <u>June 26, 1948</u>: Berlin Airlift began. More than 200,000 flights flew in food, coal and industrial goods for 2.5 million Berliners. At high point Airlift planes were landing and taking off from Berlin every three minutes.

(5) <u>May 12, 1949</u>: Soviet Union ended its blockade of West Berlin. Instead of causing division amongst German, Berliners and Allied Forces (the Airlift participants) it brought them together.

(6) <u>September 30, 1949</u>: the Airlift continued to this date to build a reserve in the event of another Soviet Union blockade.

In the many talks I've given before the Berlin Airlift Veterans Association (BAVA), the Berlin Airlift Historical Foundation (BAHF); and other groups, I have always mentioned my firm belief that "the Berlin Airlift saved Germany for Germans and helped to keep the Free World free!" It is my opinion had the Berlin Airlift not been successful, the Soviet Union would have taken over Berlin and in turn all of Germany. If this happened, the Soviet Union would have had the German industrial might and manpower under its strong-arm-communistic-control and would have been able to subjugate the rest of the Free World. Many look upon the Berlin Airlift as "the first battle of the cold war with Russia that was won without firing a shot."

Though the Berlin Airlift was a team effort at all levels, it was the determination, organization and inspiration of *four* individuals in leadership roles that were miraculously brought together at the right time, right place with the right know-how to bring about a successful conclusion..

(1) General Lucius D. Clay was the US Military Governor of Germany when Berlin became blockaded. His request to send an armed convoy to break the blockade was rejected by President Truman for fear it might start a war with the Soviet Union. General Clay felt all of Europe would be lost if the Western Powers were forced out of Berlin. He believed the future of democracy demanded they stay. General Clay was concerned that providing survival needs to a city by air alone had never been done before; plus the hardship Berliners would have to bear might be too much for them. He confided his concern to the West Berlin Mayor Ernst Reuter. It is said Ernst Reuter's response to General Clay was, "You worry about the airlift; I will take care of the Berliners." With this assurance, General Clay ordered the Berlin Airlift to begin. This as aforementioned was the greatest humanitarian operation ever undertaken by the military.

(2) Ernst Reuter, Mayor of West Berlin, who was highly respected, helped provide the morale of West Berliners that was vital. He realized the importance of working with the Western Allies but didn't forget to remind Berliners to have pride in themselves. In his speeches he let people know they weren't only fighting "against" something, they were also fighting "for" something!

Mayor Reuter's famous speech delivered before 300,000 Berliners on September 9, 1948 was inspirational.

"People of the world, people of America, England, France, Italy! Look at this city and admit that you may not and cannot betray this city or its citizens!...We have done our duty and we will continue to do our duty. People of the world, do yours! Help us at the time ahead—not just with the rumble of your aircraft engines, not just the means of transportation which you send, but also by standing firmly, as indomitably for those common ideals which alone can guarantee our future and yours! People of the world, look to Berlin! And people of Berlin, you can be certain, we want to win this battle and we will!"

(3) Major General William H. Tunner who was experienced in organizing cargo transporting flights over the Hump, the Himalayas, from India to China during World War II and later in Korea, was given charge of the Combined AirLift Task Force. General Tunner wanted precision and rhythm of flights into and out of Berlin. To obtain this required the same type aircraft, first the C-47 and then the C-54 flying in, getting unloaded and flying out. If for any reason a pilot couldn't land on the first attempt, there was no second chance allowed. The fully loaded aircraft had to return to its place of origin. In so doing many crashes were avoided. General Tunner, who was the world's foremost expert in organizing large amounts of cargo being transported in planes from one point to another; was the third individual who was part of the Berlin Airlift leadership team united to perform a task thought by many to be impossible to accomplish.

ADDENDUM of the three above:

General Lucius D. Clay – After four years of research I found that General Clay was buried at West Point Military Academy in New York State. On the day Germany was reunited, October 3, 1990, I held a lone ceremony at his grave site. The ceremony included my placing a wreath and other items including my printed words thanking him for saving Germany for Germans and helping to keep the Free World free. The English translation of an epitaph engraved in German on a separate stone at General Clay's grave site stated, "WE THANK THE SAVIOR OF OUR FREEDOM – 1978 – CITIZEN OF BERLIN."

I traveled approximately one thousand miles to present General Clay's son, a retired USAF General with the gift-wrapped "35th Anniversary of the Ending of the Berlin Airlift" Memorial Plate as requested by the Berlin lady during one of my vigils at Checkpoint Charlie. In addition, I presented a similar Memorial Plate that I designated as the Johanna Hoppe Award for an individual, organization or government that had done something very outstanding to help Berlin or Berliners. I felt no one better met the criterion of the Award than his father, General Lucius D. Clay, Sr., and this was a presentation made posthumously to his father. He happily accepted and said he would give it to his brother who was a retired US Army General.

Mayor Ernst Reuter – One might wonder if the Airlift could have been successful without him. In discussing Mayor Reuter, Henrik Bering in his book titled "Outpost Berlin" states, "During the Nazi era, Ernst Reuter had twice been sentenced to a concentration camp, and twice sentenced to death, but his life had been saved through efforts of charitable organizations in the United States and Britain that put pressure on the Nazi government. Instead, he had been permitted to leave Germany and go into exile. He spent the war in Turkey trying to assist Germans, many of them Jews, who were fleeing Hitler."

General William H. Tunner – Though firm and stern, General Tunner had the respect of all those involved in the Airlift. Several veterans of the Airlift told me that before General Tunner took charge, the Airlift was like a carnival. Not only did he get more and more survival needs to Berliners—he organized the operations of the Berlin Airlift in a manner that saved lives of Airlift participants too. They held him in the highest regard. His quest for more and more tonnage earned him the nickname, "Ten Ton Tunner." He had other nicknames too, e.g., "Willie the Wip" as Ann his widow mentions in the audio-visual documentary titled, "Berlin Airlift" that is produced and directed by Robert Frye. She said "the General was everywhere during his 12- to 14-hour day trying to get the most out of everyone."

A continuation of previously mentioned "FOUR" in leadership roles that were miraculously brought together at the right time, right place with the right know how to bring about a successful conclusion.

(4) It wasn't the Berlin Airlift pilot **Gail Halvorsen's** rank that put him in as one of the "four" who were of high leadership importance. Of the three above, two were generals and one was a mayor. At the time he was only a Lieutenant in the USAF. Gail Halvorsen, now a retired Colonel of the USAF, became known as the *"Berlin Candy Bomber," "Uncle Wiggly-Wings," "Schokolade Flieger,"* the *"Chocolate Bomber,"* and is revered throughout Germany—especially among Berliners and anyone associated with or who have an interest in the Berlin Airlift. He dropped little parachutes laden with candy and gum for the children of Berlin on his landings at Tempelhof Airport with flour and other survival needs the Berlin Airlift was providing.

Halvorsen states in his book, *"The Berlin Candy Bomber,"* the idea of dropping candy from his Airlift plane began one hot day in July 1948. He got into a conversation with about 30 children between the ages of eight and 14 near the fence who were watching the airlift planes coming in over the houses one after another. He was highly impressed by the maturity of children so young who expressed their appreciation for what the airlift was doing. They had been through the bombings of Berlin during World War II and then saw what living in terror was like when the Russian soldiers came into Berlin at the war's end. This became even more obvious as other Allied Forces entered the city and Berliners traveled both ways across the East and West borders as the Berlin Wall was yet to be built.

Berliners had an opportunity to see and compare living under communism. They were willing to endure suffering all the hardships of the Soviet Union's Berlin blockade for the right to be free. The freedom the Berlin Airlift would provide them was looked upon as being even more important than the flour. They were concerned that the winters in Berlin are brutal and hoped the Berlin Airlift would continue the means for their survival so they could go beyond this period to a time they would be free.

They so appreciated what the Airlift was doing for them. Gail said, "these were children between the ages of eight and 14 expressing such mature views."

Halvorsen waved his hand good-bye and began walking to the jeep that was to take him back to his plane. He turned and went back to the children as he remembered he had two sticks of gum, something they hadn't seen in years. As he got closer, he broke the two pieces into four and wondered if he was doing the right thing thinking a mad scuffle might be created to get one of the pieces. Much to his amazement no such thing happened. The four that got one of the pieces of gum gave the paper wrappers that the gum came in to the other children. Each child that got the wrapper ripped off a small piece and passed the remainder of the paper to others then put the piece they had to their noses to get the aroma of the gum. They then put the small piece of paper away as though they just received a deed to the world's greatest riches.

Halvorsen was so impressed by their enthusiasm with two sticks of gum that he told the children to look for him flying into Berlin the next day as he would drop little parachutes with candy for them. They were happy but asked how would they know his plane among all the planes in the Airlift. He told them he would wiggle the wings of his plane to let them know. The same number of children were there the next day as he wiggled the wings of the plane and dropped the small parachutes with candy and gum attached.

As time went by, more and more children were waiting for the parachutes with candy that the *"Berlin Candy Bomber"*—or as he was also called, *"Uncle Wiggly Wings,"* the *"Schokolade Flieger,"* and the *"Chocolate Bomber"*—was dropping for them. On one occasion, one of the parachutes almost hit a reporter from the Frankfurter Zeitung newspaper who probably was at the location because of the happiness this gesture was creating among more and more children.

The reporter wrote a story about the thoughtful actions of Gail Halvorsen, the "Berlin Candy Bomber" and the fact that this was the first happiness the children had in years. The rest is history as the story went throughout Europe and found its way to the shores of the USA. More and more individuals and organizations helped in providing candy and material for parachutes. The morale produced in this period of hardship by the "Berlin Candy Bomber" was a huge factor in bringing about cooperation, appreciation and belief the Berlin Airlift would keep them free.

Gail Halvorsen is idolized by all who know him. While in Berlin, Germany for the May 12, 1997 48th Anniversary of the Berlin Airlift, I met a Berlin lady named Mercedes Wild at Berlin Airlift Gratitude Foundation ceremony in the Tempelhof Airport Auditorium. Mercedes as a child had written to the "Candy Bomber" asking him to drop a parachute with some candy at her house. She said he would know her house as she has chickens in her yard. When Gail Halvorsen couldn't find her house as he flew in, he mailed her the candy. In time they met and to this day are the best of friends. On occasion when Gail Halvorsen and his wife Alta are in Berlin, Mercedes Wild has had them as guests. While in New York City I met a very mature German man who was a child in Berlin during the blockade. At my mentioning the name of Gail Halvorsen the *"Candy Bomber,"* the man's eyes opened wide and he told how he and other Berlin children enthusiastically watched the airlift planes come in. When they saw the wings on a plane "wiggle" and the door on the plane begin to open, the children would put a finger in their mouths to moisten it then raise it high so they could feel which direction the wind was blowing. Then they would run to the direction the parachutes were expected to land.

It is my pleasure and honor to have known Gail Halvorsen as a personal friend for eleven-and-a-half years at the time of writing. He is so sincere and so highly thought of that once when his name was mentioned in a conversation, Fred Hall, who participated in the Airlift as a Flight Engineer and presently an active member of the Berlin Airlift Veterans Association and the Berlin Airlift Historical Foundation, said of Gail, "I have never heard a bad word said about him."

Gail Halvorsen is the epitome of sincerity. Most of the finer details mentioned above were taken from his recently revised book, "The Berlin Candy Bomber." I highly recommend his book not only for what is written and its extraordinarily large number of photographs but in addition one cannot help but be affected by the obvious sincerity of such a rare individual.

The leadership and cooperation of Americans, British, French and Germans working as a team was needed if the Airlift was to succeed. This was certainly obtained.

The British played a vital role in the Airlift's success. Without the leadership and cooperation of the British, the Airlift would never have succeeded. They agreed to act under the single leadership with America's

General Tunner as the Commander of the Combined Airlift Task Force and a British officer as Deputy Commander.

The difficulties of the Berlin Airlift caused loss of 78 lives: 31 Americans, 39 Britains and eight Germans. It was an all out effort with essential teamwork vital if success was to be accomplished.

The French not having any aircraft to speak of did allow the needed Tegel Airport to be built in its zone of occupation. With the help of 19,000 Germans, Tegel Airport was built in a matter of months. This is another example of team work. In addition, the French *without permission* blew up two Soviet Union radio towers that were more than 200 feet high and a danger to airlift plane landings and takeoffs from Tegel Airport. The Germans whose lives and freedom were at stake did all they could to help the Airlift succeed.

CHAPTER 2
Anna Maria & Severino DiCocco

MARRIED BY REGISTRAR AS REQUIRED BY LAW IN GERMANY. THIS ON SATURDAY EVENING, OCTOBER 4, 1952 AND THEN IN ANNA MARIA'S PARISH CHURCH SUNDAY MORNING.

Questions to and answers from:
Mr. Severino DiCocco

Severino felt his upbringing gave him an appreciation of and importance of good morals, tolerance, religion and hard work. His wife-to-be, Anna Maria, was of the same religion and had similar likes and dislikes. Today they are still very much in love and active in their church and community.

When and where were you born?

October 20, 1927 – Guardiagrele, Abbruzzo, Italy

Were you raised on a farm, in a village, city, suburbs, etc?

On a farm.

How many were in your family and composition of same?

Four: Mother, sister, brother and me in that order (father was already in the USA to establish residence).

Was your family structured in a strict, moderate or loose manner?

I would say it was strict.

What amount of formal education did you acquire?

I was the first in the family to complete High School and the only one to receive any college. I have a total of 118 hours of college credits plus an Associates Degree in Electrical Technology.

How, generally speaking, did all or any particular part of the above affect your adult attitude prior to and during your Berlin Airlift assignment?

I believe that it gave me an appreciation of and importance of good morals, tolerance, religion, and hard work. We did not expect anything for nothing. My father came to the USA on four separate occasions. First time when he was a teenager around 1903 and in May 1926 when he decided to stay here, establish residency for citizenship, and send for his family in 1933. I was born five months after he came here in 1927.

When and under what circumstance led you to become a member of the military?

We were living on a small farm of 50 acres which had been an abandoned peach farm. It was all grown up with underbrush and some trees up to about ten inches in diameter. On some days the whole family would be out there clearing the land so we could plant crops. We originally had only one horse to help us with the heavy work. Then a few years later we had two horses and finally we got an old used Fordson tractor which was later replaced with a used McCormick Deering tractor. In 1943, my father bought a brand new International Farmall tractor with rubber tires and several different attachments so that the tractor was used for several different types of work. My brother still has this tractor and we still use it when I help him make hay.

Sometime after World War II started, my father got a job as a janitor at the nearby General Motors plant which had been converted into Eastern Aircraft Company which produced the Navy Torpedo bombers. In fact the plane that President Bush was shot down in was made here.

My brother is two years older than I am and he was working at a large dairy farm in addition to helping out on our farm. The draft board kept after him; and he certainly did not want to become an infantryman, so he tried to join the Navy but was rejected due to having flat feet. First time he found out he had bad feet, but it never seemed to limit any of his activities. So in order to avoid the draft, he volunteered and served in the Merchant Marines. He made a number of trips across the Atlantic in providing war supplies to our allies.

I felt like most of the work on the farm was dependent upon me and when we were caught up with our work, I frequently helped two different large dairy farms with their work. Many days I would be out before sunrise and still out in the field as late as midnight. Shortly after I graduated from high school in June 1945 and I turned 18 that October, I became concerned that I also could be drafted because our farm was not large enough to exempt me from the service. I had to register for the draft and was actually drafted and told to report for induction on December 22, 1945, but President Truman gave everyone who was scheduled for induction between December 20th and January 20th a reprieve, so I did not report for induction until January 24th, 1946. The first week I was in the US Army; but a week later I was sent to basic training in the US Army Air Force which of course became the US Air Force in September 1947.

What were the factors that led to your Berlin Airlift assignment?

I changed my military status from that of a "draftee" with no specific discharge date to "Regular Army" for 18 months and I was discharged on July 30th, 1947. I went back to work for a farm equipment company and later went to work for Young's Rubber Company, maker of Trojans condoms in Trenton. I was an electrician helper and liked the work helping a Navy veteran electrician. The boss (head electrician) was also a Navy veteran and much older, but he stayed mostly in the shop working on pet projects for the company owner and his two sons. I learned quickly and many times I was sent out to work on my own. Many times the Maintenance Foreman would come around and question who I was helping and I would tell him no one and that I was working alone and he would give me heck. I would tell him that I was doing whatever I was told to do and was able to do.

About one year later, the Russians blockaded Berlin and shortly thereafter I began receiving letters from the US Air Force about needing me and that I could re-enlist specifically for Operation Vittles and be assured of being assigned to Germany. The electrician I worked with the most and I were doing mostly all the work in the plant and we both felt we deserved more money than we were getting. We were both told that would only happen if the head electrician either quit or died and neither of those was about to happen anytime soon. So I felt I was in a dead-end position and no prospect of more money.

The Air Force kept bugging me and I rather enjoyed my previous one-and-one-half years of service, so I decided to make it a military career and re-enlisted in the Regular Air Force on December 28, 1948 for Operation Vittles. I sailed for Germany in February and arrived at Rhein Main Air Base near Frankfurt/Am in March 1949. I remained in the Air Force, serving mostly in airlift cargo organizations, until I retired as a Personnel Manager, Chief Master Sergeant, on February 1st, 1975. My last two years I was with the Headquarters Command, USAF Inspector General Team as Personnel Inspector.

What was your rank and duties?

Sergeant, Personnel Specialist.

What were the living conditions at your base?

At first we were in quonset huts at Rhein Main, then pre-fabricated one-story barracks; and after the Airlift was over, we moved into new masonry buildings, but for only one month because we had to go to Korea in July 1950.

What were the living conditions of the German people at the time?

Very bad. I was at the "Replacement Depot" in Marburg, Germany for about a week. The first morning we were standing outside in formation I saw a Catholic nun behind the mess hall *(where the soldiers eat)*, holding her habit up on her right arm and she had her whole right arm in the garbage cans "fishing" for any chunks of food she could find, especially meat. I guess depending on the size of the meat, they would either eat the meat, but more likely use it for making soup since the nutritional value would go much further. That scene really hit me and I suppose that I will never forget it.

Then as I began going off base and into the city of Frankfurt, I saw all the bombing damage. The glass top of the main Bahnhof was all gone, the area around the Cathedral was all leveled and throughout the city nothing but huge piles of ruins, even women and children picking through the debris sorting out whole bricks, etc. The Cathedral itself was still standing but all the windows were blown out. I felt that God must have extended his hand and not let any of our bombs hit directly on His house. Seldom did I see people on the streets laughing or having a good time. It seemed very sad that in the midst of all this our GIs were having a good time in the bars and I very seldom went into them. I felt a lot of sympathy for the people.

Give a more indepth elaboration of the first five questions. Describe your inner feelings towards the German people.

I certainly did not feel this way towards "Germans" before I joined the service. In 1943 I was supposed to make my "Confirmation" in my Church. My God-Father was in the Army in North Africa and after discussing the situation with his parents and writing to him, it was decided that his father would stand-in for him (proxy) for my Confirmation which was on October 17th, 1943. Shortly after that my last letter (V-mail) to my Godfather was returned to me with "KIA 9 Sept 1943." He was killed during the Allied landing on the beach at Salerno, Italy. He was born in Italy, the same as I was, and here he had been killed there. I was shocked at this news and I realized he had actually been killed before I was even confirmed. I was angry as hell toward the *Germans* and swore that somehow I would avenge his death. But by the time I arrived in Germany, a lot of my anger had dissipated although I was still a little leery. I even thought that if the (Germans) found out I was an Italian that they might harm me because Italy abandoned Germany during the war. But as it turned out everything was all right even though a few times I felt I was disliked by the Germans because here I was, an "American" occupier, especially when I started dating a German girl and we would be walking around town.

It has been said Germans were starving in some areas while the military poured gasoline on many loaves of bread and burned them because they were stale. Did anything of this nature occur where you were assigned? If it did, what feelings did you have?

I personally did not see this. (See question above that asks, "What were the living conditions of the German people at the time?")

What was the general attitude of the American military and German people toward one another when you were first assigned there? If tense, when did it change, if it did, and what were some indications you noticed?

I have already mentioned some of this above. But there were many Germans working with the Americans on Rhein Main Air Base. My wife was originally hired by the Americans as an interpreter at a small Army base between Frankfurt and Wiesbaden waiting for the runways, etc, to be repaired and opened at Rhein Main. Besides clerical, building maintenance, auto and aircraft maintenance, there were some professional Germans also. I remember I went to the Dental Clinic for a check-up and was taken care of by a German woman dentist. First time I ever saw a woman doctor. I think that most Germans realized the need and value of the humanitarian work we were doing in keeping Berlin free and I think that most of them were working together as a team very well. We even had a Labor Battalion at Rhein Main who were Polish DPs (displaced persons) and I felt there may have been some ill feelings between them because the Germans felt they needed the work, etc. Also, the opportunity for the black market provided many contacts with the local Germans. The GI made a little money and the Germans got something they needed at a reasonable cost. Even the American authorities sort of closed their eyes at much of this. I have spoken to a number of Germans since then and I was told that the black market was a very important contributing factor toward the quick recovery of Germany. But there were always a few GIs and Germans who would never really accept each other.

When did you first see or become aware of your wife-to-be?

My wife-to-be was a secretary to our Troop Carrier Group Commander at Rhein Main and I was a Personnel Specialist in one of the Squadrons under the Group. We frequently spoke to each other on the phone on military business matters. I asked around about her and I never heard anything bad. I liked the sound of her voice and then I was at the Group Headquarters and someone pointed her out to me. I liked what I saw. In addition to our contact on official matters, I began to get a little more personal and asked for a date and I was put off a couple of times. Finally, she told me she needed a ride home and I took her. We then made a date to go to Wiesbaden and had dinner at a local restaurant. We found an American Thrift Shop there where they sold used clothing and she bought a good cloth overcoat which she still has. It has been re-lined twice since then.

What was your first impression when you saw her?

I thought she was attractive.

When did you begin to realize you were falling in love?

Probably around April to July 1950.

What were some of the outstanding highlights of your courtship: where did you meet, how did you meet (was it difficult to get passes from the base), where did you go, was there any negative reaction from Germans seeing the two of you together?

At first her parents were not too happy about her dating an American GI and an Italian but they warmed up to me, and by the time we got married, they were great to me. We dated once or twice a week. We would go to the American movies and Enlisted Club. I had a car (shipped from the USA) and would go for rides around the country side and visit interesting places. We would stop by some stream and wash the car and just talk and listen to the music on the radio. We would visit one of her aunts who ran a Gasthaus about an hour's ride away. We would go shopping or sightseeing in the Frankfurt and Wiesbaden and other nearby towns. This only lasted for about six months, because the Korean War started and in July 1950 our entire Troop Carrier Group (with three squadrons of C-54's) was ordered on temporary duty (TDY) to McChord AFB, Washington for 30 days for the purpose of flying troops and supplies from the States to Japan. That 30 days was extended to 90 days.

We were there for five months until December 1950. We all expected to return to Germany, but instead, we were ordered on further TDY to Japan. There we flew troops and supplies such as fuel, ammunition, bombs, etc. into Korea including very austere landing strips near the front lines. During my free time from my Personnel duties, I frequently accompanied our air crews on many of these flights and helped unload our cargo. I had done the same thing on the Berlin Airlift. I was not the bar-hopping type, so I occupied my free time by flying and helping to do a job that needed to be done.

In October 1951 our status was changed from TDY to permanent change of station (PCS) from Rhein Main Air Base to Ashiya Air Base in southern Japan, about 75 miles across the water from the southern tip of Korea. As a result of this change in our status, Air Force Regulation made all of us eligible for immediate rotation to the States. Finally in March 1952 we started getting replacements and we were individually returned to the States. I came back in April 1952. That means that we were in a TDY status from July 1950 until October 1951—15 months total. During the Persian Gulf war there was an outpouring of sympathy for our "poor GI's" because they had to be gone for a couple of weeks. How times do change!

It is also interesting to note that when we left Rhein Main and went to McChord AFB, there were about six guys in my squadron who were planning to marry German girls. One guy even had his papers in, but when we got to McChord, he married a local girl there. I was the only one who actually returned to Germany to get married in October 1952—after a separation of 26 months.

When and where did you propose marriage? Did she accept your proposal at the time? What was your reaction?

We corresponded at least several times a week, sometimes daily, and we would tell each other all sorts of things—news, jokes, poems, how we missed each other and felt about each other. A number of times we each felt we were just dreaming about ever seeing each other again and commented that maybe we should forget about each other. But then the next letter cheered me up and kept me going and the same thing happened to her. We would write about getting married but it just kept being put off for no reason.

One time I must have written and said something about being married, and she wrote back and said something about how did I know she would marry me because I never asked her. So in my next letter, I asked and she responded with a yes and I was real happy about it while at the same time I was quite apprehensive, not knowing if I would get permission, how would I get back to Germany because I certainly did not have the money (had less than $1,000 to my name), and of course everything that goes with getting married, living with a woman, and becoming a father, etc. My father gave me $250 when I returned to the States after getting married.

What was the reaction of your military friends when realizing you had fallen in love and intended to marry a local German lady?

Nothing overtly, but several of the officers—mainly my commander, although not openly hostile—did nothing to help me overcome legal and paperwork problems.

What was the reaction of her parents, relatives and friends upon learning she was in love and accepted your proposal of marriage?

I never had any hostility from her parents, brothers, uncle, aunts or cousins, even while dating.

What were the official requirements for marriage? Were obstacles put in your way and if so, why? How long did it take before you were officially married?

I had to have written permission from my Squadron Commander and Air Force Headquarters in Europe. Part of the documentation was she had to have a medical clearance from the American consulate, permission to travel, and I had to have a statement from my father in which he guaranteed that I was able to support her and she would not become a public burden. (If we still had this in effect now, we would not have such a big problem with so many illegal immigrants being on welfare.) These problems were compounded a hundred times because we were in Japan and we had none of the regulations with which I had to comply with in Germany. I asked my commander for help, and he told me that I was the one who wanted to get married—not him. In other words, no help from him.

My bride-to-be sent me copies of the applicable regulations and we started our paper work. When I thought we had everything, the American consulate in Frankfurt denied her application for a visa because they believed she had tuberculosis. She was checked at the Air Force Hospital in

Wiesbaden—she was okay. Finally when I returned to the states from Japan, I contacted my local Congressman and asked for his help. I next heard from my bride-to-be. The American Consulate sent a staff car to pick her up for another interview.

She said when she walked into the Consul's office, he had nothing on his desk except one stack of papers with a big red "Expedite" cover on it. He merely expressed his regret at her supposed bad health and hoped that she would make it to the States before getting sick and signed her papers. I guess she was that random number that they had to disapprove, but our persistence paid off. What was so ironic and made me so angry was that the Consulate was approving visas for hundreds of "war-brides" who were "displaced persons" and there was no way anyone could check on the backgrounds, etc.

My bride-to-be was born and had lived in the same town near Frankfurt/Am all her life and worked for the American military since 1945, including classified information, and they were bound and determined to keep her out. WHY? The more resistance I got, the more determined I would be. A Lieutenant Colonel who was in the Air Force's Congressional Liaison office in Washington helped me get leave orders to visit Germany and also got me one of the VIP planes to Germany. That was the same organization that now flies the President and politicians around the world. So we married on October 4th, 1952—26 months after I left Rhein Main in July 1950.

Where were you married? Describe such things as the setting and who attended.

We first were married by the Registrar in Schwalbach/Taunus which is required by the law in Germany. This on Saturday evening, October 4, 1952 and then on Sunday morning in my wife's parish church in Niederhoechstadt/Taunus. In addition to her large extended family some of our close friends both German and American attended. On our honeymoon we visited some of my relatives in my home town in east central Italy in addition to Venice, Italian Riviera, Naples, Pompeii, Rome, Pisa, Genoa, Milan, Switzerland, etc. We even climbed Mr. Vesuvius!

What adjustments were made in performing your military obligations as a married man?

I now knew that I was responsible for someone other than myself but did my job and went wherever the military sent me. I was fortunate to have a wife who understood *military life.*

When and where did you return to the States? Was it direct from your Berlin Airlift assignment or from additional foreign service elsewhere?

Sent TDY from Rhein Main to McChord AFB, Washington for 30 days which lasted five months then further TDY to Japan—from July 1950 to April 1952 supporting the Korean War effort.

How did you help your bride adjust to being in the US? Did she speak English?

She spoke English very well and I do not think that our way of life was that much different from hers, except for living where the war was.

Were relatives and neighbors friendly to her and did they go out of their way to make her feel welcome? Did anyone ever give her a difficult time?

I do not think that anyone, my family or friends, did anything to not make her feel welcome. Maybe a couple of times they may have asked her questions that possibly made her feel a little uncomfortable to answer.

Describe how through the years your bride's adjustment developed.

I think she adjusted quite well—as I said we were not that different in our ways of life. Not like if she had been oriental. She liked Italian food, and she learned to cook many different dishes (not just Italian).

Do you have children? If so give an indepth elaboration.

Mr. Severino Di Cocco can proudly answer this question but prefers giving the honor to the love of his life, Mrs. Di Cocco.

Has your wife returned to Germany to visit her relatives, either alone, or with you and/or with your children? In turn have her relatives been here?

Yes many times, read Mrs. Di Cocco's response for an elaboration.

Why are you so proud and happy that the love of your life became your wife?

I believe we had many things in common, same age (she is five months behind me), same religion, same likes and dislikes. She understood military living and accepted more than her share of responsibilities as a wife and mother and took charge whenever I was gone. We always made whatever decisions that needed to be made together. We were as "one" in dealing with the children. She always made me feel I was important to her and took care of me in many ways; and I love her immensely.

Questions to and answers from:
Mrs. Anna Maria (Bopp) DiCocco

Mrs. Anna Maria (Bopp) DiCocco as a young school girl believed the Nazi propaganda which was heard and read in the papers, radio and taught in her school. She thought the German military was so strong it would conquer the world and take revenge for the hardship placed upon Germany after World War I. As the war progressed, she began to realize she had been wrong in believing Hitler was good for Germany.

When and where were you born?
    1928 — Niederhoechstadt/Taunus.

Were you raised on a farm, in a village, etc.?
    In a village.

How many were in your family and composition of same?
    Four — Mother, Father, Brother.

Was your family structured in a strict, moderate or loose manner?
    Fairly strict.

What amount of formal education did you acquire?
    Eleven years...high school diploma.

What was the economical and political atmosphere in Germany and how did it affect your immediate family and others both near and far?
    Before the war, as best I can remember, the economic situation in

Germany was good. My father had been out of work for five years before Hitler came to power. By building roads, and as we later learned, starting on his war machine, everybody who wanted to work had a job. My father was a Master Car Mechanic, and he started to work for Opel. He joined the National Socialist German Labor Party (National Sozialstische Deutsche Arbeiter Partei – NSDAP), the Nazi Party. He firmly believed that Hitler was the best thing that happened to Germany, since he brought Germany out of the depression and generated work. My mother was just the opposite, and so were my grandparents. Most of my father's friends were of his persuasion, but some were not, and there were no hard feelings, just some very lively discussions as to who was right.

How did all or any particular part of the above affect your adult attitude prior to, during, and immediately following the war's end?

I stuck with my father. Having had a certain amount of Nazi indoctrination in school, I was convinced my father was right, and everybody who was against Hitler was a traitor. I remember my father taking me to Frankfurt the day after "Kristallnacht." I very vividly remember the Jewish stores being looted; clothing, bedding, sheets and towels hanging on trees outside the stores; glass and china broken in the streets; and the synagogue burning. I could not understand what was happening and why, since I was only ten years old, and we knew a Jewish merchant who used to come to my grandmother's house to sell his goods (my grandmother was a seamstress) and this Jewish merchant was a party member. He supported Hitler, and now he had lost all he had. As I grew older I questioned more, and by the war's end I realized that it had all been a big mistake.

When did you and others begin to feel Germany would be in war? Was this looked upon with favor and/or fear?

In the summer of 1939. Being a child, and believing that the world was against us, I and my fellow students were *convinced* that war was the best way to conquer the world and live happily ever after. In the summer of 1939, we children played a math game, which told us when the war would begin. The answer to our game was 1.9. 1939, which meant 1 September 1939. And, dumb kids as we were, we couldn't wait, and sure enough, on 1 September 1939, German troops invaded Poland and the war began. I kept a scrapbook of all the German victories, and with a lot of others, was convinced that it would be over in no time, that the whole world would give in and give us what we wanted.

Did the war's early victories cause a feeling of euphoria—that Germany was so powerful no country on earth could stop it?

Yes, definitely.

What were some of your home front war time activities in the early stages of the war?

None, I was too young.

How long a period of time transpired before it was realized the war would take longer for Germany to win than expected?

I don't remember exactly (it has been a long time—55 years) but I think it was around 1943 when most of the battles had slowed down, the German Army had taken over much of Europe and North Africa and everything seemed to have come to a stand-still. We still believed that eventually we would win the war, but it would take a long time.

What was the general feeling when Germany opened the Russian front? How did this affect your home front activities?

When the German troops invaded Russia, we were told that the German government had intercepted Russian intelligence reports to the effect that Russia was ready to invade Germany. Of course we believed it, and since German troops were so victorious in the beginning, we again thought the world was ours to conquer. Only later did I realize that if Russia had been ready to invade us, the German troops would not have been so victorious. There was no change on the home front. From the very beginning everybody had to help. Women without children had to work in factories. Women with children had to help out on the farms. Quite a few women who never wanted children before became pregnant very fast.

One way it affected us was the son of very good friends who came home on leave before being sent to the eastern front. He was 18 years old. We never saw him again. We later learned that he was taken prisoner in Stalingrad, and died in a prison camp in Siberia. A cousin of mine was taken prisoner in Stalingrad also and came home from a prison camp in Siberia four years later.

Did bombing or fighting take place where you lived? If so, to what extent?

Our village did not suffer any damage, some bombs fell outside in the fields. I went to high school in Frankfurt, and on one of the bombing raids, Frankfurt was hit extremely hard. We had gym class when the air raid sirens went off, and had to run to the shelter in our gym clothes. Our school was totally destroyed. I still remember the smell of burning houses, the dead bodies, all the ruins, and trying to get home after the *all clear*. My parents knew of course that Frankfurt was hit hard, they even knew that the section of town where my school was had been hit, so you can imagine their joy when I arrived home after walking through rubble and burning houses to get out of Frankfurt, and then the five or six miles to my home.

One day I rode my bicycle to my aunt's home about 12 to 15 km from my home. She had a restaurant, and we used to bring her vegetables from our garden. I had planned to stay a few days and help her. (It must have been vacation time). The air raid sirens went off when I was still half a mile or so from her house. There was no shelter, and there was a sign to that effect on the road. I heard airplanes and saw fighter planes coming, low and shooting. I must have jumped from my bike into a ditch on the side of the road three or four times. I got to my aunt's house, put my bike into her barn, and ran across the street into the shelter.

I no sooner got into the shelter when the bomb hit my aunt's house. Of course we did not know where the bomb hit until the *all clear*. The bomb hit the barn which was right in the back of the kitchen. The kitchen was destroyed. My bike was in the front yard facing the other way from where I had put it. My aunt's goat was on top of the rubble with only the head sticking out, but still alive. Thankfully, no one was injured. It was a small bomb, but big enough to do a lot of damage.

Again I had to walk home, since the bike could not be pedaled. I could sit on it to go downhill, but uphill and on straight-aways I had to push it. Another time my brother and I walked to my aunt's home through the fields and over the mountain. My brother was only about ten years old. I was about 16 (give or take a year). My aunt had a dog that my brother loved dearly, and when it came time to go home, my brother decided to take the dog. I could not talk him out of it, so we took the dog without my aunt's knowledge. Halfway home we had another air raid. We were in a forest, so we just decided to keep going. But the little dog would not move. So we had to stay. All of a sudden there were more airplanes, more shooting and we heard bombs. Then came the *all clear,* and the dog came willingly. Had the dog not balked before when we wanted to keep going, we would all have perished. The bombs that we heard fell right on the path we were on; half a dozen craters, one after another. The dog saved our lives...I call it a miracle.

Towards the very end, the men left behind were to report for military duty. My father left with the rest of the men still at home. Since my father worked for the Opel Werke who by this time was manufacturing war machinery, he was exempt from military duty. But this order meant everybody. So they all left, and we had no idea if and when we would see them again. But lo and behold, by evening they were all back. My father said they were to be issued weapons, but no uniform. He was told that he would be shot if he did not obey orders. He told them to shoot him, and he left. The others left with him. As the Americans came closer, there was shooting.

Food supplies were getting short, and wherever there was something to be had, we went to get it. I was a daredevil and spent a lot of time in ditches when the artillery shells whizzed by—all for a loaf of bread and a pound of butter. To me it was an adventure. When the American tanks finally rumbled through our village, it was with a sigh of relief that the fighting and shooting and bombing was finally over, and also a measure of sadness, because we had lost the war and been betrayed by our leaders.

What effect did the war have on everyday living, e.g., shortages, attitude, travel, etc.?

During the war there were no shortages in food, since I lived in the country and we had our garden, chickens, goats, pigs. The shortages most experienced were in clothing and shoes. The attitudes were mixed, depending on political views.

When and how did you hear of the Japanese attack at Pearl Harbor and the US entry into World War II?

I do not remember.

What were the thoughts and impact of Germans to the US entry into the war?

Another enemy to beat.

What was the general opinion of Germans to the US prior to World War II?

I don't think we thought much about it. I really don't remember.

As the war progressed what was the general opinion of German civilians to the American military who were fighting the German Military? Also, how did German civilians feel the American military involved in combat would treat them at this time?

To us (the Germans), the Americans were the enemy. Once in a while we would see the American airmen who were shot down and captured being brought to prison camps. I would have liked to have talked to them, since I was learning English in school, but was afraid to do so. We were also told if and when the Americans came, they would kill the men and rape the women. So of course we were afraid.

Was the Russian military anywhere near your home area?

No.

As the war progressed what was the general opinion of German civilians to the Russian military who were fighting the German military? Also, how did German civilians feel the Russian military, involved in combat, would treat them at this time?

Not applicable.

Did your area receive much war damage? Explain the extent to people and property.

Answered in aforementioned question that asked "Did bombing or fighting take place where you lived?"

When did it seem assured Germany would lose the war? What were the outstanding fears of the apparent loss?

After the Africa Corps was pushed back, the allies landed in Italy and pushed the German Army back, the invasion in Normandy was another blow to the German Army, and on the Russian front the German Army had to retreat, most Germans realized that it was over. Some people hoped for a miracle, but most knew that for all practical purposes, it was over, it was only a matter of time.

What was the reaction when the war ended and Germany lost? Was there general dissension or cooperation among your neighbors

regarding the loss at this time?

Sadness because we had lost the war, but we were glad that the war was over.

What were the conditions in your area when the war ended? Were there shortages of vital needs? What were the outstanding fears of the apparent loss?

There were food shortages, everything...shoes, clothing was in short supply. The black market flourished.

What was the feeling towards the American military when the war ended and they occupied the area—if they did? Were the occupiers friendly and considerate or were they to be feared?

To us (the Germans), the Americans were the enemy. We were also told that if and when they came they would kill the men and rape the women.

What were some of the outstanding things the American military occupiers might have done that had you appreciate them or vice-versa, fear them?

Give us their surplus food instead of burning it. They put gasoline on loaves of bread and burned it because the bread was stale while we were so very short of food. (*Author's note: Henrik Bering states in his book* Outpost Berlin, *"Initially, US troops viewed the Germans as Nazis and Krauts. There were to be no dealing with them whatsoever...The US troops were under orders not to throw food into the garbage because the Germans might pick it up. Anything discarded had to be doused with gasoline. Few* soldiers obeyed the order." Mr. Bering also mentions because of the ban on fraternization US troops were not supposed to talk to Germans. This proved to be impractical as the US troops and Germans began working together.)

Describe the tension that both sides probably had towards each other and how this tension in time eased. What factors led to the easing of tension? Did the Americans help the local economy by making purchases of items or assorted types of services?

It was just a matter of time for tension to leave. One day there was a knock on our door and three American soldiers were standing there with towels and soap. They asked if they could take a bath which my mother said yes to. They were very friendly and before leaving thanked my mother and asked if they could bring their clothes to her for laundering which they would pay for. She said yes. After the soldiers left we agreed, "they were really nice." They had left their wet towels and bar of "Cashmere Bouquet" soap that had such a pleasant fragrance. The soap impressed us tremendously as we only had the hard plain soap we made ourselves. The soldiers must have gotten transferred as we never saw them again, but they were the type of factor that helped in the easing of tension.

When did you first see or become aware of your husband-to-be?

Sometime in January 1950 in the office where I worked.

What was your first impression when you saw him?

He was just another GI.

When did you begin to realize you were falling in love?

After he was transferred, in the summer of 1950.

What were some of the outstanding highlights of your being courted: where did you meet, how did you meet, were you working at the time, and where did you go?

I started working on the American Air Base in the Fall of 1945. I wanted to return to school and become a journalist, but the schools were closed, and in order to eat we had to get a ration card, and to get a ration card, we had to work. The interim German Officials were under US jurisdiction. Since food was scarce, and jobs were plentiful, one could not sit at home and expect to be fed. The Americans needed workers and the German cities needed to be rebuilt, etc.)

I spoke English, I could type and take shorthand, so I was assigned to the Americans. I worked in Group Headquarters. Severino (my husband-to-be) was at the Squadron level. We talked on the phone on business matters quite often. He also had to come up to Group Headquarters every so often, and I guess he saw me.

The first time he called and asked me for a date, I did not know who he was and I refused. He was persistent and the next time he asked for a date I had seen him, knew who he was, and I needed a ride home. So I accepted his invitation. Things progressed rather slowly, since I couldn't "figure him out." We would go and play bingo once a week, and on Sunday he would pick me up and we would drive around, mostly to see some of the nice places in the area, like Heidelberg Castle, or the castles along the Rhein River. When the weather got warmer, we did a lot of hiking in the

Taunus mountains. We would pack a picnic lunch and head for a different place every Sunday. That is when I realized he was really "one of a kind." He was nice, considerate, and not like some of the other guys I had gone out with that I had to fight off, who only had one thing in mind, and that was sex. So my affection for him grew, and I realized that he also really liked me for what and who I was to him.

All that came to a screeching halt in June of 1950 when the whole organization was transferred from Rhein Main Air Force base to a base in Washington State to support the Korean War effort. That is when I realized that I loved the guy, and I guess he realized that he loved me. We wrote letters every day, hoping he would return soon. But the weeks turned into months and the months into years before I would see him again.

When and where did you receive a proposal of marriage? Did you accept the proposal at the time. How did you feel—what was your reaction?

The proposal came in a letter. As I said in the paragraph before, we wrote letters every day. Sometimes one of us would get real discouraged, and wonder if we should forget each other, but thank God we never felt that way at the same time. We started talking about marriage, and I remember saying in one of my letters that "here we are, talking about marriage, but how do you know that I will marry you, you haven't asked me yet." In answer to that letter came the proposal, which I accepted.

What were the reactions of your parents, relatives and friends upon learning you were in love with an American military man and accepted his proposal of marriage?

My parents wanted me to be happy, and they would rather have me happy many miles from home than unhappy living next door.

What were the official requirements for marriage? Do you feel obstacles were put in the way and if so, why? How long did it take before you were officially married?

The requirements to get married were stringent. We could not get married and live in Germany. Military Regulations, issued by the US Army in Europe (they had administrative jurisdiction over all the US Armed Services) stated that US military personnel could not get married to German nationals until three months before rotating to the US. Germany was not a sovereign country yet, as we were still considered an "occupied" nation. (I believe Germany was granted total sovereignty around August 1955.) These regulations did not change until sometime in the mid 50's or later.

His Commanding Officer had to approve the papers, and he was not in favor of anyone of his troops marrying a German. I had to undergo a physical at the American Embassy and they would not approve it. I had always considered myself healthy, but the Embassy Official insisted that I had Tuberculosis. It took many months to get it all straightened out, and after writing letters for 26 months and overcoming many obstacles, with the help of my husband-to-be's congressman, he returned to Germany and we were married in October 1952.

Where were you married? Describe such things as the setting and those in attendance.

We were married by the Registrar in Schwalbach/Taunus, as is the law in Germany, on Saturday evening, 4 October 1952, and then in my parish church in Niederhoechstadt/Taunus on Sunday morning. I had a large extended family, many cousins, uncles and aunts, who all came to the wedding, and then some close friends, both German and American. We went on a three week honeymoon to Italy, and upon our return, he had to return to the United States and I remained in Germany until I received my visa to join him. I came to the States in February 1953, on a Navy vessel, leaving from Bremerhafen, and after ten days docking in New York, where my husband was waiting for me.

If married in Germany what adjustments did you have to make to be with your husband? Where did you live, etc.?

Answered in previous question.

Where, when, and how did you go to the States?

Same as above.

Did you speak English when you arrived? How were you treated and how were you helped to adjust to the new country? Did your husband's relatives and friends go out of their way to be of help and make you feel welcome?

I spoke English, I had no trouble adjusting, and I was accepted by my husband's family and friends. We did not live near his family, since they were in New Jersey, and we lived in Massachusetts where he was stationed.

Describe how through the years your adjustment developed.

Since my husband remained in the military we moved around a lot.

And me, being a gypsy at heart, I loved it. Some assignments were not as nice as others, but we always made the best of it, and I knew when I married him what I was getting into. I made friends easily, and everywhere we went, we encountered other German brides. I had no problems adjusting at any time.

Do you have children? If so give an indepth elaboration regarding their births, upbringing and present status.

We have five children, three daughters and two sons. They were born in Massachusetts, New Jersey, France, Texas, Maryland. We had twin boys in Texas, but lost one when he was two days old. We brought them up fairly strict, the way we were brought up. They all did well in school, and four have gone on to college, and the two boys have graduate degrees.

The two boys are Air Force Officers. The oldest son went to the Air Force Academy, and received his Master's Degree in Astronautical Engineering from MIT. He is a Lieutenant Colonel in the US Air Force. He is married and has three children.

The younger son went through the Corps of Cadets at Virginia Tech, and got his Master's Degree from Dayton University in Aerospace Engineering. He is a Captain, soon to be Major in the US Air Force.

Our oldest daughter lives in Italy at the present time and does not work. She got her Bachelor's Degree from Catholic University in Washington, DC. Before she moved to Italy with her husband two years ago, she managed the computer network for Arlington County government.

The next daughter is a Budget Manager for the Naval Research Lab in Washington, DC. She is married and has three children. She had no desire to go to college but rather go to work, and she has done well for herself. And our youngest daughter went to West Chester University in Pennsylvania and received a degree in Micro-Biology. She works in Clinical Research.

So we feel blessed. Our children have done well, and so far we have six grandchildren. Our youngest son, and our youngest daughter are not yet married.

Have you ever returned to Germany to visit your relatives? If so, were your husband and children with you? In turn have your relatives visited you in the States?

We were stationed in France for four years, and had many opportunities to visit Germany, and my family visited us quite often. Also, in the 60's we were stationed in the Azores, and visited every summer. Since my husband's retirement from the Air Force in 1975, I have returned to Germany every summer for a month until my mother passed away in 1989. My father had died in January 1975. I would take one of the children with me now and then, and the children have visited by themselves. My mother visited us once in 1978.

Why are you so proud and happy that the love of your life became your husband?

I love my husband very much, we've had our ups and downs like everyone else, but I cannot imagine a better husband. I am proud of what he has accomplished, and is still accomplishing. We have had a wonderful and happy 45 years together, and hopefully will have many more.

Photo taken in Sacramento, California at the September 1997 reunion of the "Blackjack Squadron." (Squadron participated in the Berlin Airlift.)

November 1992 Family Photo. (Standing L-R) Christine, Caterina, Marc, Marie Luise and Ricardo. Parents, Anna Maria and Severino are seated.

CHAPTER 3
Eva & Paul Hawkins

OFFICIAL MARRIAGE 28 JULY, 1951 IN THE CITY OF BERLIN AT 3PM. THEN MARRIED AT THE BASE CHAPEL AT TEMPELHOF BY CHAPLAIN ONE HOUR LATER AT 4PM.

Questions to and answers from:
Mr. Paul Hawkins

On their first date Paul told Eva she should get no ideas — that he wasn't going to marry a German girl. She asked what made him think she would marry him anyway! In time Paul couldn't leave Germany without Eva the girl he had fallen in love with.

When and where were you born?

    1928, in Harrisville, West Virginia.

Were you raised on a farm, in a village, city, suburbs, etc?

Harrisville was and still is a small town about 1200 population. When I grew up small farming was the main industry and some oil and gas.

How many were in your family and composition of same?

I had two sisters when I was born, I was the third of a total of six. However, my youngest sister died at birth. My brother didn't come along until 1937, so there I was totally dominated by girls. My third sister was two years younger than I.

Was your family structured in a strict, moderate or loose manner?

My family was structured rather moderately for the times. My sisters and I each had our chores to do. They were more strictly controlled than I. Most of the discipline was carried out by our mother but generally when dad took a position that was it. He was considerate. For example; he asked me if I would milk the cow before he decided to buy it. I remember when I was about ten years old, he sat me down and told me he would buy cigarettes for me if I wanted to smoke because he was afraid that I would smoke corn silks. He thought smoking corn silks could cause a person to get yellow jaundice.

What amount of formal education did you acquire?

Immediately after high school I attended one semester of college at a college about 60 miles from home. I paid for myself but after one semester I had no more money. I joined the Army Air Force to get the GI Bill after three years of service. I was discharged from the USAF July 28th, 1957. I entered West Virginia University as a Sophomore. I received a Bachelor's

Degree in German Language and Literature in May 1960. We moved in August to Louisville, Kentucky where I enrolled as a beginning seminarian at Southern Baptist Theological Seminary. I earned my Master of Divinity Degree in January 1964. This was for the purpose of getting the required education to serve as a military chaplain. Unfortunately the services didn't need a chaplain 36 years old with a wife and four children. I served as a full time pastor of Calvary Baptist Church in Oak Hill, West Virginia for a year and a half. Then I returned to West Virginia University to work on a Master's Degree for the purpose of teaching German Language classes at the University. I earned my Master's Degree in German in 1967. I had already been teaching at the Parkesburg Branch Campus for two years, so I went there full time.

How, generally speaking, did all or any particular part of the above affect your adult attitude prior to and during your Berlin Airlift assignment?

I entered the Army Air Force in February 1947. During my high school years we were at war with Germany and Japan. Even in our small rural West Virginia setting the war was with us. We did some very silly things as I look at it now. But it was these kind of things that put the whole country behind the war effort. For example, we had black out drills, air raid wardens, and helpers. The Boy Scouts went around to make sure no light was showing for the bombers to see. Today I think what bombers? From where would they originate. What would they find in a small town in the foothills to bomb?

We had several young men in Europe and in the Pacific fighting the war. Many had left school before graduation, some had been killed over in Germany. Somehow all of this made a keen interest in me for Germany. When I enlisted, I was asked where I would like to go if I had to go overseas? I replied, "Germany." The sergeant laughed and said we are bringing guys back from Germany, pick someplace else. I said "No!" He asked and he had my answer. In October 1948 I arrived in Berlin.

When and what circumstance led you to become a member of the military?

This question was answered previously.

What were the factors that led to your Berlin Airlift assignment?

I was assigned to a Holding Squadron at Camp Kilmer, New Jersey along with 1000 other personnel. We were awaiting assignment to the Dew Line in Canada above the Arctic Circle. Five of us were trained in maintenance of the AN/CPS-5 Median Range Search Radar. Apparently the military leaders in Berlin decided that this radar was the one to place on the building in Tempelhof Airfield, Berlin. It was to be modified to be an Air Traffic Control. It was modified for moving target indication and was the first of its kind anywhere.

What was your rank and duties?

I, along with my four colleagues, arrived in Berlin with the rank of Private First Class.

What were the living conditions at your base?

Living conditions on base were essentially good, better than most of us had experienced in our military careers so far. Many parts of Tempelhof had been damaged by the Russian Armed Forces as they withdrew for the western parts of Berlin. Why did they do this damage? My assumption is that they didn't want to turn over anything to Americans and other allies since they wanted full control of Berlin. When we insisted that they keep the agreement, they tried to keep us from using what they could. I remember we first lived in the area facing Tempelhoferdamm. The area under the eagle on Eagles Square was unusable. They later worked on the area along Columbiandamm and we moved our living quarters there.

Food was good. I learned my first German words in the chow line. Only one woman on the serving line spoke and understood English. She would take the order in English and tell the other ladies on the line what to put on the trays in German. For example; most of the soldiers would order meat and potatoes and no vegetables. She would say, "Fleisch und kartoffeln ohne gemuse."

What were the living conditions of the German people at the time?

Living conditions for the German population were very bad. This was November after the Airlift had begun in May 1948. There were no lights in the streets. Each section of the West part of Berlin had two hours of electricity per day. Most of the time it was in the middle of the night. Food was scarce. It was cold and fuel also had to be flown into the city. People heated only a small part of their apartments and took cold baths. Some apartments had two or three families living in them. It was a very hard time.

Describe your inner feelings towards the German people you encountered at the time.

I don't remember ever feeling that the German people were my enemy. As I came into contact with the cleaning people, the mess attendants, the German workers on the installation of the radar tower, and the piano player in the lounge, I saw them as other people in my world at that time, and respected them for what they did.

It has been said Germans were starving in some areas while the military poured gasoline on many loaves of bread and burned them because they were stale. Did anything of this nature occur where you were assigned? If it did, what feelings did you have?

It would be hard for me to believe that this sort of thing happened in Berlin. I never saw or heard of this. I did see the elevator operator go around the building and strip the cigarette butts and put them into a can. He somehow reused the tobacco. I saw GI's throw candy and bubble gum out of the window onto the street for the children. Most people knew the difficulty of the Germans at that time and had compassion for them.

What was the general attitude of the American military and German people towards one another when you were first assigned there? If tense, when did it change, if it did, and what were some indications you noticed?

The status of Americans in Germany changed in early 1949 when the Americans stationed there were no longer called *"occupation forces."* I was attending a special air force management school at Camp Lindsey, Wiesbaden when the change came about. If I remember correctly, we were briefed about the change in status. Before the change, the Germans one met on the street tended to move to the side to let the military person walk by. After the change, many of the German men would hold their ground and make you move from one side or the other. We had been warned that any problem caused by a confrontation with the Germans might provoke an international incident. The implication was that this would not be good for us personally.

When did you first see or become aware of your wife-to-be?

My roommate and colleague, Tim, had become acquainted with a German girl. This girl had a sister and they were to have a New Year's Eve Party. Tom's girl's sister had a friend and they needed someone to pair with her at the party. Tom invited me. I hesitated because I was to meet a British girl at the service club that night. I finally agreed to go with Tom on the blind date. The blind date was my wife-to-be. We met at that party.

What was your first impression when you saw her?

She was very beautiful. She was reserved. She really didn't want to get out of bed to come to the party. We went to her apartment and begged her. I told her that night that she should get no ideas; that I was not going to marry a German girl. She told me, "What makes you think I would marry you anyway?"

When did you begin to realize you were falling in love?

About half way through the evening, I asked her if I could see her again. She didn't answer. As we parted she asked if I was coming back. I knew then that she hadn't understood what I asked before. We dated regularly after that. She had a two-year-old daughter I knew that I was in love when I couldn't stand the idea of leaving the two of them in Germany.

What were some of the outstanding highlights of your courtship: where did you meet, how did you meet (was it difficult to get passes from the base), where did you go, was there any negative reaction from Germans seeing the two of you together?

A.   There were not very many restaurants that we could use on the economy. First, they had enough problems feeding their own population, so why add more? Second, I think the Berlin Military Post Headquarters didn't have enough people to check out the cleanliness of all the restaurants, so they allowed only those restaurants which had been checked, making the rest off-limits.

We spent most of our time together walking in the park or shopping along the street. I had no trouble getting off the base. I would take the streetcar to the S-Bahn and then ride to the next stop and walk to the apartment. I remember one night we went to the operetta. I could take her to the Air Base, but was afraid I would lose her to another guy. We did go to the base one time for a picnic and swim party where they served roasted marshmallows and chocolate on top of Graham crackers.

B.   We weren't concerned about Germans seeing us together but it was reported that German women were sometimes kidnapped while shopping in the Russian sector, especially if they had been seen on the streets with American GI's. They would just disappear. Also, Germans who had some value to the Russians were sometimes kidnapped right out of their homes in the Western part of Berlin.

When and where did you propose marriage? Did she accept your proposal at the time? What was your reaction?

On Thanksgiving Day 1949, approximately eleven months after we got acquainted, while in the apartment, I asked Eva to marry me. She accepted my proposal and I was very relieved.

What were the reactions of your military friends when realizing you had fallen in love and intended to marry a local German lady?

My squadron commander at first refused to even consider my request to extend my enlistment to stay in Berlin. The Airlift was over and he wanted me to leave the Air Force and return to college. We had no way of knowing that my staying in Berlin saved me from active service in Korea. My military buddies had no reaction because they were also marrying German girls.

What was the reaction of her parents, relatives and friends upon learning she was in love and accepted your proposal of marriage?

Eva's mother died when she was three, and her father was killed in Russia in 1942. Her step-mother approved of me and accepted the marriage idea. Eva's brothers and sisters also approved.

What were the official requirements for marriage? Were obstacles put in your way and if so, why? How long did it take before you were officially married?

Marriage to a German was not popular in 1945 up to the 50's. Eisenhower had been against fraternization, and there was much red tape. In general a police report had to be prepared by the German Government, a background type check by the OSI, we had to have at least one interview with a Chaplain. The Squadron Commander had to give his approval. We had a lot of papers assembled before we had the approval. The Air Force would not allow the marriage to take place until three months before my return date. We started the paper work immediately after our engagement in November of 1949. We finally got the approval and were able to get married on 28 July 1951.

Where were you married? Describe such things as the setting and who attended?

We we were married at the Standesamt in Neukoln section of the City of Berlin at 3PM. This was an official wedding. We went to the Base Chapel at Tempelhof and were married by the Chaplain Deutschland at 4PM. Our best man was the Air Base First Sergeant Templeman. The bridesmaid was his German girl friend. I had told my great aunt that when I got married I would have a good job, a house, a car and enough money to live comfortably. When we got married it was three days before payday. I spent my last $65 for the cold cuts at the reception. We had the reception in our apartment at Fulda Strasse and a good time was had by all.

What adjustments were made in performing your miliary obligations as a married man?

We, my two friends and myself were married for about a month and we were still required to maintain quarters on the base. The Squadron Commander had difficulty making up his mind. We had a sergeant in the section that we suspected was a stool pigeon. Once we proved he was we used him. We came into the maintenance office one morning complaining loudly about the Commander not allowing us to move off base. Very soon he said he had to go to the PX. We watched as he went directly to the Headquarters.

After lunch I was crossing the square and the Commander called to me. I reported to him, and he said, "Sergeant Hawkins, what is this I hear about you going to the Base Adjutant about moving off base? I told you we hadn't made up our minds."

I replied, "That is right sir, and I haven't gone to the Adjutant yet." Two days later he gave us permission to move off base. Since we had only two months before we returned, it didn't really change my military duties much.

When and where did you return to the States? Was it direct from your Berlin Airlift assignment or from additional foreign service elsewhere?

Upon return to the continental US, I was assigned to the AACS Squadron at Wright-Patterson AFB, Dayton, Ohio. Here I was assigned to all weather flight testing division of Wright Air Development Command.

How did you help your bride adjust to being in the US? Did she speak English?

Already in Germany we worked at improving Eva's English since most of our lives would be in English speaking areas. She learned how to be a real West Virginian by spending three months with my parents. When she met my sisters, they were quick to tell her how she didn't have to listen to what I said.

Were relatives and neighbors friendly to her and did they go out of their way to make her feel welcomed? Did anyone ever give her a difficult time?

Everyone seemed to accept Eva, they were friendly and did make her feel welcome. Especially my immediate family. However, it was difficult for my mother to get close to Eva until the latter part of her life. The difficulty my mother had was the normal difficulty a mother often has with the women who marry their sons. Added to that were the stories that foreign women only married GI's to get a chance to come to the USA. Eva's way of doing things was different and from a different cultural background so that led to some misunderstanding. Also the language barrier—or more so the manner of responding—created misunderstandings. No serious breaches occurred. Later in life when my mother lived alone and Eva was thoughtful and attentive, my mother came to love and appreciate her ways very much. My brother's wife, who is from England, also experienced similar difficulties.

Describe how through the years your bride's adjustment developed.

As long as I was a Sergeant in the Air Force, she seemed to know her place…I say this in jest. That is, she was rather reserved. She got along well with others but didn't feel that she was as educated as those she met. She had a hard time adjusting to my leaving the Air Force and going to school to be a Chaplain. I Pastored Churches to work my way through school. She felt out of place. She didn't know how to be a Pastor's wife. She actually did very well. She may have been a better Pastor's wife than I was a Pastor.

When I left the Pastorate and went back to school, she adjusted very well. But when our son David got her involved in distributing Shakle

Products and talking about people' health, she blossomed. She has really become what I consider the ideal Pastor's wife.

Do you have children? If so give an indepth elaboration.

We have four children. The eldest is Evelyne, born in Berlin. After graduating from high school, she became a beautician. She had some problems with the chemicals used in her trade so she changed to office work. She had her own business supplying office temporaries in Pittsburgh. She is married and now works as an Officer for Nations Bank in Richmond.

Thomas was also born in Berlin. He was an excellent student and came to within one semester of having a BA in Psychology; but he liked carpentry better, so he is now a construction contractor.

David was the third born and was also born while I was still in the Air Force. He is a person who feels deeply for other people. He owns his own natural food store and herbal consultation business. He has celebrated over 21 years of success. His mother helps with customers twice per week and I help with the Herbal preparations.

John was the late-comer. He was born while I was in the seminary. He was the only one who started and finished school in the same country. John has married and has two beautiful children. He was trained to be a communications specialist in the Air Force and works for GTE.

All our children are a blessing to us and we are very proud. All of them are proud of their German heritage and like to visit their German cousins in Berlin.

Has your wife returned to Germany to visit her relatives, either alone, or with you and/or with your children? In turn have her relatives been here?

After leaving Germany in 1951, it took me 21 years before I could afford to take Eva to visit Germany. We visited in 1972 with our youngest son. In 1971 I had a travel grant to study at the Goethe Institute, but I could not take my family. After that in 1974 to 1975. I was awarded a Fulbright Exchange to teach English in Kassel. My wife and youngest son accompanied me for the year in Germany. After that we traveled every three to four years for visits. We had a little family reunion in Berlin in the summer of 1989, just a couple of months before the fall of the Wall.

Why are you so proud and happy that the love of your life became your wife?

I feel like I cheated all the others who might have stolen her from me. We decided when we married that it would be for life. My only regret is that I have only one life with her. But we are going to make it as long as possible.

Questions to and answers from:
Mrs. Eva Hawkins

Paul Hawkins proposed to Eva on Thanksgiving Day, it was the happiest day of her life. Paul became a Pastor and Eva became the ideal Pastor's wife. She couldn't have made Paul more happy and proud. She has fulfilled Paul's life as he has hers.

When and where were you born?

I was born on March 26, 1933 in Winningen, Hinterpommern, which is now part of Poland. After World War II the Allies decided to give that part of Germany East of the Oder-Neisse Rivers to Poland and to take a section of Poland and give it to Russia.

Were you raised on a farm, in a village, etc.?

My family moved early in my life to Kolberg, a resort town on the Baltic Sea coast.

How many were in your family and composition of same?

When I was three years old my mother gave birth to twins, a girl and a boy. Both my mother and the newborn boy died. My father married again and my half-brother was born in the next year, and a half-sister followed two years later.

Was your family structured in a strict, moderate or loose manner?

My family was like most German families at the time—strict. My life as the step-daughter and the oldest of four children was not easy in any sense of the word.

What amount of formal education did you acquire?

I attended the regular Volksschule and one-half a year of business school.

What was the economical and political atmosphere in Germany and how did it affect your immediate family and others both near and far?

I came from a middle class family. As far as I remember, the economical and political atmosphere was good.

How, generally speaking, did all or any particular part of the above affect your adult attitude prior to, during, and immediately following the war's end?

I do not know.

When did you and others begin to feel Germany would be in war? Was this looked upon with favor and/or fear?

My family didn't discuss the political situation with the children. But we were afraid that our dad would have to go if war broke out.

Did the war's early victories cause a feeling of euphoria - that Germany was so powerful no country on earth could stop it?

I do not remember.

What were some of your home front war time activities in the early stages of the war?

We practiced blackouts when the sirens blew all during the war.

How long a period of time transpired before it was realized the war would take longer for Germany to win than expected?

    I don't remember.

What was the general feeling when Germany opened the Russian front? How did this affect your home front activities?

    That was the time when my dad was called up to serve. He went to Russia in 1942 and didn't return.

Did bombing or fighting take place where you lived? If so, to what extent?

    There was no bombing over our town. It was too small and there was no industry. We could hear the planes fly over us.

What effect did the war have on everyday living, e.g., shortages, attitude, travel, etc.?

    There were rations. We didn't travel far from home. But we always believed we would win the war because of the propaganda.

When and how did your hear of the Japanese attack at Pearl Harbor and the US's entry into World War II?

    I don't remember.

What were the thoughts and impact of Germans to the US's entry into the war?

    I don't remember.

What was the general opinion of Germans to the US prior to World War II?

I do not know.

As the war progressed what was the general opinion of German civilians to the American military who were fighting the German Military? Also, how did German civilians feel the American military, involved in combat, would treat them at this time?

We hadn't heard anything about the American Military, since we were closer to Russia. Somehow, we feared the Russian Army would come and capture us.

Was the Russian military anywhere near your home area?

They came closer to our hometown toward the end of the war. Rumors had it they were about to blow up the bridges that led to our town and capture it.

As the war progressed what was the general opinion of Germans civilians to the Russian military who were fighting the German military? Also, how did Germans civilians feel the Russian military, involved in combat, would treat them at this time?

As mentioned above, we feared what the Russians would do to us.

Did your area receive much war damage? Explain the extent to people and property.

Only at the end of the war. The city was 80% destroyed after my sister and I escaped. No one was to leave the city, but my sister and I asked a German unit of soldiers if they would help us get out of the city. They agreed because we didn't have a lot of luggage. We heard later that the truck that carried us was the last one that left the city because the bridges were destroyed so no one could leave. We were headed for Berlin, but on the way Russian planes attacked the unit and we had to get out of the vehicles and dig ourselves foxholes. We saw a lot of refugees on the way and lots of belongings in ditches, because people just wanted to save their lives.

When did it seem assured Germany would lose the war? What were the outstanding fears of the apparent loss?

We never believed that Germany could lose the war, even to the end.

What was the reaction when the war ended and Germany lost? Was there general dissension or cooperation among your neighbors regarding the loss at this time?

We were among strangers and no one talked about the loss. We finally made it to Berlin and arrived at our stepmother's who lived with another couple in one apartment.

What were the conditions in your area when the war ended? Were there shortages of vital needs? What were the outstanding fears of the apparent loss?

People didn't fear the Americans like they did the Russians.

What was the feeling toward the American military when the war ended and they occupied the area-if they did? Were the occupiers friendly and considerate or were they to be feared?

The part of Berlin where I lived was under Russian occupation, and we had to stand in line to get our rations. Things were pretty bad. We went hungry a lot.

What were some of the outstanding things the American military occupiers might have done that had you appreciate them or vice versa, fear them?

People didn't fear the Americans like they did the Russians.

Describe the tension that both sides probably had toward each other and how this tension in time eased. What factors led to the easing of tension? Did the Americans help the local economy by making purchases of items or assorted types of services?

The fact that Berlin Neukoeln became part of the American occupation and that the Airlift started, eased the tension toward American soldiers. Neukoeln is a section of Berlin to the East of Tempelhof bordering on the Russia sector.

When did you first see or become aware of your husband-to-be?

I met my husband at a New Year's Eve Party that I didn't want to attend, but at the coaching of my friends I went and met Paul. I spoke very little English and he almost no German.

What was your first impression when you saw him?

I really wasn't very impressed, but he asked me if he could come and see me again and so our friendship developed. I don't remember when I fell in love with him. He kept coming back to see me and my little daughter. He had told me that he would never marry a German girl. I told him, "What makes you think I want to marry you anyway?"

When did you begin to realize you were falling in love?

Paul took me to the NCO Club at the base for a 4th of July celebration. We roasted marshmallows and put them on Hershey chocolate between Graham crackers. I thought I had died and gone to heaven, not ever had I eaten anything like it. Another time we were invited to the house of his Warrant Officer and the lady served cherry pie which I had never eaten before. I wanted to impress him and make a cherry pie but we had to spit the seeds out of the cherries. On occasion we went to the club dancing.

When and where did you receive a proposal of marriage? Did you accept the proposal at the time? How did you feel-what was your reaction?

Paul proposed to me on Thanksgiving Day 1949, and I accepted. It was the happiest day of my life.

What was the reaction of your parents, relatives and friends upon learning you were in love with an American military man and accepted his proposal of marriage?

I can't remember the reaction of my stepmother when we told her, but my relatives and friends were happy for me.

What were the official requirements for marriage? Do you feel obstacles were put in the way and if so, why? How long did it take before your were officially married?

The official requirements were tough. Yes we had to overcome a lot of obstacles. I believe the American Military didn't want their soldiers to marry German women. We finally were married three months before Paul's tour of duty was complete which was the 28th of July 1951.

Where were you married? Describe such things as the setting and those in attendance.

We were first married at the German Standesamt for the Civil Ceremony which is the legal one in Germany and at the Base Chapel with only a bridesmaid and best man present. The reception was at our apartment with family and friends present. Paul had only $65 to spend on the wedding.

If married in Germany what adjustments did you have to make to be with your husband? Where did you live, etc..?

Paul moved in with me. He didn't have to go back to the base every evening. He gave me German Marks so I shopped in the German stores.

Where, when, and how did you go to the States?

We went by ship, the "SS Washington" from Bremerhaven to America in November 1951. It was rough to cross the ocean in November.

Did you speak English when you arrived? How were you treated and how were you helped to adjust to the new country? Did your husband's relatives and friends go out of their way to be of help and make you feel welcomed?

I spoke a lot more English when we arrived in the US. We went by bus to my husbands hometown in West Virginia. The roads were very crooked and I almost got sea sick driving on the bus. Paul's father greeted us when we arrived at the bus station. He welcomed me to America. We had to drive about five miles to get to Paul's home where his parents had a country store. I received a rather cool response from my mother-in-law—only a "Hi"—I felt like going right back where I came from. It was hard at first to adjust to the American way.

Describe how through the years your adjustment developed.

We moved a lot while my husband was in the service that's where I made my friends and adjusted to America.

Do you have children? If so give indepth elaboration regarding their birth, upbringing and present status.

We have four children, one daughter and three boys. Three were brought up by their sergeant dad, very strict. The youngest just the opposite. But they all turned out all right.

Our daughter was born in Germany. My husband married both of us; he later adopted her. I think he fell in love with her and married me.

Our oldest son, Thomas, who lives in Hawaii was also born in Germany. He is a successful contractor.

Our middle son, David, was born in Fairborn, Ohio while we were stationed at Dayton, Ohio. He is a master herbalist and owns a very successful natural food store called "Mother Earth Foods."

Our youngest son lives with his family in Manassas, Virginia and is working for GTE. He was stationed in the Philippines and married a Philippino woman. They have two beautiful children, ages five and eleven.

Have you ever returned to Germany to visit your relatives? If so, were your husband and children with you? In turn have your relatives visited you in the States?

I returned to Germany after 21 years. It was the first time we could afford the trip. I felt like a visitor, as the only thing I now had in common was the language. For years now we have been trying to make the trip every two to three years to visit relatives and enjoy the different parts of Germany.

Why are you so proud and happy that the love of your life became your husband?

I don't know what would have happened to me if I hadn't met my husband and if he hadn't loved me enough to go through all the trouble of marrying me. He is the best husband and father any woman could wish for. He told me when we got married, the word divorce wasn't in his dictionary.

PAUL AND EVA AT THE 1997 BERLIN AIRLIFT VETERANS ASSOCIATION REUNION IN COLORADO SPRINGS, COLORADO.

FAMILY PHOTO OF PAUL AND EVA HAWKINS:
(L-R) EVELYNE, THOMAS, JOHN, EVA, DAVID AND PAUL.

CHAPTER 4
Annie & William Michaels

BILL AND ANNIE'S CHURCH WEDDING IN YOUNGSTOWN, OHIO ON JULY 15, 1950. (THEY HAD BEEN OFFICIALLY MARRIED IN GERMANY ON JANUARY 18, 1950 BY A LOCAL OFFICIAL AS REQUIRED BY THE LAW IN GERMANY.)

Questions to and answers from:
Mr. William Michaels

Bill said when they first met that Annie told him he looked "married" and she didn't want to go out with a married man. It took him a long time to have her realize he wasn't married, and in time she became his Bride. Though Annie was called to Heaven more than ten years ago, Bill's love for her is as strong today as the day they were married.

When and where were you born?

Born in Youngstown, Ohio, 21 March 1922.

Were you raised on a farm, in a village, city, suburbs, etc.?

I was raised in a city of 250,000

How many were in your family and composition of same?

Five members in my family: parents, two brothers and myself.

Was your family structured in a strict, moderate or loose manner?

My family was moderately strict.

What amount of formal education did you acquire?

I graduated from high school.

How, generally speaking, did all or any particular part of the above affect your adult attitude prior to and during your Berlin Airlift assignment?

I was taught to take things as they come and not to prejudge the actions of others.

When and under what circumstance led you to become a member of the military?

I was drafted into the Army in 1942.

What were the factors that led to your Berlin Airlift assignment?

I was the Flight-chief of the Single-Engined Flight at Stewart Field, Newburgh, New York, when I volunteered for the Berlin Airlift in order to do "something different."

What was your rank and duties?

I was a Technical Sergeant with assigned duties as Flight Engineer on C-54, Skymaster aircraft.

What were the living conditions at your base?

Being a senior Sergeant, I was quartered in the British Sergeant's Mess. My living conditions were very good.

What were the living conditions of the German people at the time?

Celle, except for one limited air raid, was virtually untouched during the war. Buildings were intact, but the town was overcrowded with displaced persons. Rationing was still in effect. (I ordered fried eggs in a restaurant, and when I received them, I discovered they had been fried in fish oil.)

Describe your inner feelings towards the German people you encountered at the time.

I served with the Eighth Air Force in England during the war when we were trying to bomb Germany out of existence. Now we were helping them. At first it was a very strange feeling to meet these former "enemies." I became friends with several former Luftwaffe personnel and realized that the war—even though fought by persons like me—was really between Governments and not the people.

It has been said Germans were starving in some areas while the military poured gasoline on many loaves of bread and burned them because they were stale. Did anything of this nature occur where you were assigned? If it did, what feelings did you have?

I did not witness any action against the civilians.

What was the general attitude of the American military and German people towards one another when you were first assigned there? If tense when did it change, if it did, and what were some indications you noticed?

The attitude between the American military and the German people was quite friendly at Celle and remained that way during my tour.

When did you first see or become aware of your wife-to-be?

As I stated in "A Love Story," I first saw Annie in a cafe in Celle.

What was your first impression when you saw her?

I was greatly attracted to her but felt that I had no chance with someone like her.

When did you begin to realize you were falling in love?

I realized that I loved her at first sight.

What were some of the outstanding highlights of your courtship: where did you meet, how did you meet (was it difficult to get passes from the base), where did you go, was there any negative reaction from Germans seeing the two of you together?

The most memorable highlights were being together, holding hands, walking along the Aller River and just enjoying each other's company. We went to the civilian movie theater and cafes and both military and civilian clubs. I cannot remember any negative reactions from Germans who saw us together. My duty schedule consisted of 12 hours on and 24 hours off-duty. During duty hours, we usually flew three round trips to Berlin. The 24 hours off-duty made it possible for us to spend much time together.

When and where did you propose marriage? Did she accept your proposal at the time? What was your reaction?

I proposed on April 10, 1949 at the second table along the right-hand wall of the Cafe Wilhausen in Celle where we were having Butter-Cream Cake and coffee. She accepted. I was on cloud nine.

What was the reaction of your military friends when realizing you had fallen in love and intended to marry a local German lady?

My military friends were very pleased for me, and whenever I had to be away for several days, they looked after her.

What were the reactions of her parents, relatives and friends upon learning she was in love and had accepted your proposal of marriage?

Her parents were unsure. I think they felt that I would leave and not marry her.

What were the official requirements for marriage? Were obstacles put in your way and if so, why? How long did it take before you were officially married?

Official requirements were: permission from the commander to get married, pre-marital medical examination by military doctors, and others I cannot remember. Obstacles were not put in our way—they just happened. I took a seven day leave in July, 1949, shortly after I asked to be relieved from flying duty. This request was made to allay a fear caused by a dream Annie had. She dreamed of an in-flight fire on my aircraft during my duty shift which resulted in a crash causing the death of all aboard.

We were on the way to Cologne for me to meet her relatives when an accident occurred which left her in a hospital in Bielefeldt with a smashed right thigh. I stayed with her until my leave had expired. Several days after returning to Celle I received orders assigning me to the States. I was unable to get a cancellation of those orders or a delay. I returned to the States.

We corresponded, made plans, and in December 1949, I returned to Germany to get married. Annie was in a full-body cast and was unable to travel to Frankfurt, in the US Zone of Occupation, for the required medical examination. After several trips to Frankfurt, I got the medical forms required for completion of the exam by a British Military Medical Officer. The doctor of a British Armored Brigade seemed very pleased to help us. A snag was encountered when we were told that the wedding could not take place at home but must be held in the City Hall—no exceptions.

Since my leave was up in several days, we decided to have the party on our hoped-for wedding date. The local city official who had previously told me that the ceremony had to be conducted in the City Hall, arrived at the house with an interpreter and marriage documents in German and English. We were married with Annie's family and friends in attendance on January 18, 1950.

Where were you married? Describe such things as the setting and who attended.

(This was included in the answer immediately above.)

What adjustments were made in performing your military obligations as a married man?

I can't remember that any adjustments were required.

When and where did you return to the States? Was it direct from your Berlin Airlift assignment or from additional foreign service elsewhere?

I returned to the States directly from the Berlin Airlift and was assigned to Chanute AFB, Illinois with duty as an Aircraft Engine Instructor.

How did you help your bride adjust to being in the US? Did she speak English?

I suppose I helped her adjust by always being ready to fully and patiently try to answer any questions she might have, and by taking her to places where she would meet people. She spoke very little English when she arrived in the States. TV Soap Operas helped her associate words with actions.

Were relatives and neighbors friendly to her and did they go out of their way to make her feel welcome? Did anyone ever give her a difficult time?

My friends and relatives were more than friendly in greeting Annie and in making her feel wanted. With the exception of one family in our neighborhood, all our neighbors treated Annie as a friend. The exception was an Air Force family living next door to us. The father, mother and teenage son, upon seeing Annie alone in our yard, would give her the NAZI salute, shout, "Sieg Heil" and tell her to go back to where she came from. When I finally confirmed this action, I contacted the General commanding the base. He told me that he would not have such actions on his base. He read the riot act to the husband and transferred him to a remote duty site.

Describe how through the years your bride's adjustment developed.

She became active with the Boy Scouts and organizations helping the needy and really became more "American" than most native born Americans. She was most proud of becoming an American citizen.

Do you have children? If so give an indepth elaboration.

We have two sons we adopted after Annie had several miscarriages that the doctor said was probably due to the harsh and inhuman treatment she suffered while in a concentration camp. Both boys are PhDs and are successful in their fields.

Has your wife returned to Germany to visit her relatives, either alone, or with you and/or with your children? In turn have her relatives been here?

Annie's family immigrated to the US in 1954. Her parents are both gone. Her brother lives in Illinois.

Why are you so proud and happy that the love of your life became your wife?

We had 37 wonderful, fulfilling years together before her death on the last day of 1986.

ADDENDUM: William R. Michaels

Bill notes in his "A Love Story" that he and Annie could not have been married before his leave was up in Germany without the outstanding help by the British Army Unit.

Annie's father Hubert Kirschbaum, whom Bill called *"Pappa,"* being a Catholic opposed the Nazi Party, because he felt it was a Godless organization. He helped allied airmen escape capture during the war.

Hubert had a long distance hauling business with four ten-ton trucks in operation before the war. Two trucks were taken away from him early in World War II when he refused to join the Nazi party. When he still refused, another truck was taken away. One day he had a neighbor with him when going to Cologne to clear away rubble from a night time air raid. He was stopped by a Luftwaffe officer who drafted, him, his truck and his neighbor into the German Air Force. He with his truck was assigned to make deliveries to married officers from the commissary. Now his family had a little more to eat as he managed to take small unnoticeable slices from sausages or pieces of food from this or that.

Pappa became involved with the German underground while stationed in Helmstadt and helped allied airmen escape capture. He was responsible for assisting 12 allied airmen; two whom he spirited away from the base stockade and took to his home until able to move them. He told Bill several of the escapees had written letters describing his part in their escape to be given to the Allied force so that he might be given special treatment if needed in the future. Pappa always kept their letter on his person.

Bill had always listened but had doubts that the stories were true until while celebrating Christmas Eve in 1949 there was a knock on the door. Three South African Air Force airmen were there with gifted-wrapped packages for Pappa and Mutti, Annie's mother, and wishing them a Merry Christmas. They could not thank them enough and confirmed that Pappa had given them shelter (one even said Pappa sneaked him out of the base stockade). They couldn't thank him enough! When the British swept across Northern Germany, the family was living in Celle. Upon being ordered to evacuate his apartment, Pappa showed the Provost Marshal the letters from the airmen and was permitted to stay in his apartment.

Questions to and answers from:
Mr. William Michaels for Mrs. Annie Michaels

Annie was called to Heaven on December 31, 1986 after she created 37 wonderful years of happy marriage for her Bill. Though this author never met Annie, I know for certain she exists in Bill Michael's heart to this day. He cherishes every moment they had been together.

Annie was opposed to what Hitler was doing and in her position as a Luftwaffe Teletype Operator "accidentally" sent coded messages to wrong addresses. She was charged with espionage and sent to a concentration camp where she went from 120 pounds in weight down to 70 pounds.

Only questions Bill feels he could answer for his beloved Annie are listed. Extracts from a booklet entitled, "A Love Story" that Bill Michaels wrote about his Annie follow the questions.

When was Annie born?
November 23, 1923, in Cologne, Germany.

Was she raised on a farm, in a village, etc.?
Early years were spent with her grandmother in a village north of Cologne.

How many were in her family and composition of same?
Father, mother and in 1937 a brother.

Was her family structured in a strict, moderate or loose manner?

Very strict mother; moderate father.

What amount of formal education did she acquire?

I believe that girls went to school until the age of 14.

What was the economical and political atmosphere in Germany and how did it affect her immediate family and others both near and far?

Everybody was affected by the tremendous rate of inflation that often took a day's wages to buy a loaf of bread. (That is, if any bread was available.) People had to evade gangs of communist and socialist bullies who roamed the streets looking for trouble. Her father would warn them when trouble could be expected and they would remain behind locked doors.

How, generally speaking, did all or any particular part of the above affect her adult attitude prior to, during, and immediately following the war's end?

It instilled a sense of thrift and a hatred of violence.

When did she and others begin to feel Germany would be in war? Was this looked upon with favor and/or fear?

Her father who was in the trucking business realized that the high overpasses and shallow grades of the Autobahn were not required for motor vehicles but were ideal for armor and other heavy military equipment and told his family that a war was being planned. His family had suffered deaths and wounded family members in World War I; and he did not want to go through that experience again.

Did the war's early victories cause a feeling of euphoria—that Germany was so powerful no country on earth could stop it?

Her parents were not followers of Hitler and could not see how it was possible for Germany to conquer the world. They expected the worst.

What were some of her home front war time activities in the early stages of the war?

She gathered scrap metal, rags, and other materials as stated by the authorities.

What was the general feeling when Germany opened the Russian front? How did this affect her home front activities?

The people felt that it was a huge mistake. Enthusiasm flagged when the losses from the Eastern Front became known. The truth became known by listening to the forbidden BBC news broadcasts.

Did bombing or fighting take place where she lived? If so, to what extent?

Cologne was very heavily bomb-damaged. Three apartments in which they lived were damaged to the point of being unlivable. At one time the building collapsed and she was trapped in the basement and had to be dug out.

What effect did the war have on everyday living, e.g., shortages, attitude, travel, etc.?

There were shortages of almost everything. Travel was restricted to extreme emergencies and military. The attitude of the people changed to a concern of getting by.

What were the thoughts and impact of Germans to the US entry into the war?

The feeling in her family was that the war would be lost but also the hope that America would help Germany against Russia.

What was the general opinion of Germans to the US prior to World War II?

The general feeling was that the US would not fight a foreign war.

As the war progressed, what was the general opinion of German civilians to the American military who were fighting the German Military? Also, how did German civilians feel the American military, involved in combat, would treat them at this time?

Being under aerial bombardment day and night, the American Military did not rate high marks. However, the civilians believed they would get treated fairly by the Americans.

Was the Russian military anywhere near your home area?

No Russians were nearby.

As the war progressed what was the general opinion of Germans civilians to the Russian military who were fighting the German military? Also, how did German civilians feel the Russian military, involved in combat, would treat them at this time?

The civilians felt that the Russian Army could be beaten but if not, the Russian Militia would be very harsh.

Did her area receive much war damage? Explain the extent to

people and property.

Cologne heavily damaged as previously mentioned above.

When did it seem assured Germany would lose the war? What were the outstanding fears of the apparent loss?

Unknown. They feared that they would receive the same treatment from the Allies as they did after World War I.

What was the reaction when the war ended and Germany lost? Was there general dissension or cooperation among her neighbors regarding the loss at this time?

Following the loss, a high level of cooperation was experienced with trying to get a decent living.

What was the feeling towards the American military when the war ended and they occupied the area—if they did? Were the occupiers friendly and considerate or were they to be feared?

Her family was in the British Zone of Occupation. She worked as a cook for a detachment of Military Police.

When did she first see or become aware of her husband-to-be (you)?

When I entered the Cafe—where she was with friends.

What was her first impression when she saw you?

She always told me I looked "Married."

Where, when, and how did she go to the States?

She arrived at La Guardia Airport on the 4th of July 1950.

ADDENDUM: William R. Michaels

William R. Michaels (Bill) has so much love stored in his heart for Annie that he felt by writing "A Love Story" about their love, it would make him feel she is here. Most of the following information has been obtained and paraphrased from the aforementioned booklet.

In 1949 Bill was a Flight Engineer aboard C-54 's flying food and fuel into blockaded Berlin. He received a long awaited three-day pass and expected to use it to read, rest and just be lazy; but his roommate arriving late from a flight, asked Bill to go to town with him in the event his date was no longer there. Bill gave in and said yes; but if the date was there, he would make a fast reverse and return to the Base.

When they got to town, the date had given up on him but was still there with three of her girlfriends. They insisted on Bill staying a while and having a drink with them.

Annie was one of the girls. It was love at first sight. He saw her sitting with her friends and suddenly felt awkward and strangely shy. There was no logical reason for him to feel this way. He was 27 years old and had been around. But never with a person who so completely overwhelmed him. She was introduced to him as "Mitz" Kirschbaum. He tried desperately to make a date with her, but she insisted that she would not "date a married man." Nothing he said seemed to change her belief that he was married. She said he "looked married." The ice was finally broken with Bill continually insisting he wasn't married plus they found that friends each knew had been trying to get them together as they felt they would be a perfect match. After that Bill spent all his free time in Celle with Annie.

Bill's meeting with her family went extremely well; he felt totally accepted. After meeting with her family, Bill was told she would prefer being called by her given name "Anna" instead of her nickname "Mitzi." Bill immediately changed it to "Annie."

Annie had a very difficult childhood. The first home she remembers was an abandoned railway carriage that had no water, gas or electricity. Once a week she and her parents went to a public bathhouse for a complete bath. Meals were cooked on top of a kerosene heater and clothes cleaned by boiling them in a large tub over an open fire.

This was a time of extreme inflation in Germany. She told Bill she remembers standing in line with her mother for hours in front of a bakery to buy a loaf of bread only to find when they reached the head of the line that her father's pay from the day before would not be enough for a single loaf of bread. In addition to their being hungry, they lived in constant fear of the roving bands of political hoodlums—both communists and National Socialists, who were out looking for a fight.

Annie's father, who is discussed in further detail in the first half of this chapter, had refused to join the Nazi party, because being a Catholic, he said he could not give support to a Godless organization. One day Annie came home from school wearing a school-provided Hitler Youth Uniform. She had never seen her father so angry. He ordered her to remove the uniform at once, and never to let him see her wearing it again!

Krystallnacht and the book burning by the Nazis were etched in her memory. There was a small neighborhood grocery store that was owned by the Jewish parents of one of her best friends. Annie remembered the store windows being broken, the stock being destroyed, and her friend and parents being severely beaten by the Brown Shirts. Shortly after midnight, a truck stopped in front of the ruined store; and the following morning her friend and parents were no longer there and never seen again.

After completing schooling, Annie was assigned to work as a servant to a couple who owned a café. It was a government requirement for all graduates to work outside the home to prepare for adult life. She became a Nurse's Aid in 1940 and was able to save her food rations and pay for her parents. During the stay at the hospital, she contracted diphtheria, and since *"miracle drugs"* were not yet in existence, she had a very hard time with the illness and almost died.

She told Bill how her family would secretly listen to BBC news on the radio on the bed and under the blankets with the volume very low so the sound could not be heard. Anyone reported listening to the BBC was arrested and many persons were reported by their *friends and neighbors.*

In 1943, Annie was drafted into the Luftwaffe and became a Teletype Operator for supply. She disliked being in the Air Force and the way her father had been treated, and began to make mistakes in transmitting messages. These *"mistakes"* were traced to her and she was charged with espionage and found guilty.

At the local jail, Annie and the other prisoners were told they would never be free again. She was sent to a forced-labor camp in Altona, near Hamburg where there were approximately 600 political prisoners. Manual labor was enforced from dawn until dark or thereafter. They would be sent to Hamburg for rescue work and bomb damage clean-up after air raids. They were ordered not to speak to anyone. The civilians they helped were told the prisoners were "volunteers" from other countries who did not speak the German language. If prisoners received gifts, the guards would keep them for "safe keeping."

Annie told Bill instances of unbelievable cruelty and hardship. When their children would hear her speak of some of the lesser suffering she experienced, they would feel she was making up the stories. How could any human be that heartless to another human they thought.

Everything done in the camp was at double time with beatings by guards for lagging. Breakfast consisted of a thick slice of hard, black bread. This was the only bread provided for the day and had to be kept on one's person for fear of it being stolen. The main meal for the day was usually potato soup made by boiling potatoes, complete with dirt and other debris, to make a fairly thick consistency. The soup was ladled into the prisoner's metal container which also served as a urinal after the buildings were locked for the night. Very often bodies of grubs and other insects would be floating on the surface of the soup. Some of the girls would trade bits of bread for them. Annie told Bill she could not bring herself to eat insects. On rare occasions they would be given a very thin stew with shreds of meat and the usual insects, and coffee brewed from acorns.

Annie went into the camp weighing 120 pounds and was less than 70 pounds when she obtained her freedom.

Not all guards were brutal. One woman guard who often entered the barracks after the day's work was over cleaned the girl's injuries and sometimes would bring cigarette butts for girls who smoked. This guard died as a prisoner in the camp after a girl who didn't smoke reported her.

A World War I Veteran, in the "Home Guard" uniform, was sometimes assigned to guard Annie's work group. He always put on a show of brutality, prodding the girls with his rifle or hitting them with the rifle stock when they might be seen by other guards, especially SS guards. Upon reaching work sites, he would let the girls work leisurely and usually would have pieces of boiled potatoes or bread for the girls. One day he slipped Annie a piece of paper and whispered that if she and any of her friends could escape, they should go to the address on that piece of paper. She memorized the address and disposed of the paper even while wondering if it was a trick.

One day the work groups weren't formed and the voice of the Adjutant was heard over the loudspeaker saying the gates were open and everyone was free and should hurry home. It was a trick, and machine guns positioned at each side of the gate began to cut down those who rushed through the gate!

Annie and two other girls ran as fast as they could, dodging and jumping over the dead and wounded. The three girls were fortunate to reach a clump of bushes and hid beneath them. The guards stopped at the last body which was just a short distance away from where they were hiding. When it got dark, the three went to the address Annie had memorized that the guard had given her. A large grandmotherly type woman greeted the girls and welcomed them into her home. She was the wife of the guard who had given Annie the address. She and her husband fed and nursed the girls until they gained strength. The girls were given money and a change of clothes and sent on their way. The three girls reached Celle where Annie's parents were living.

Years later when Bill was courting Annie, Annie had a horrible dream about Bill's plane crashing. She kept on insisting that Bill not fly in the plane! Because of her fear and the fact Bill had flown 170 flights, Bill asked to be temporarily removed from flying duties. His request was granted. Shortly thereafter, the time he would have been on duty shift, his plane had an in-flight fire and crashed. All aboard were killed. Annie's dream came true and she had saved Bill's life.

Things couldn't have been going along any better for Bill and Annie. They were making plans to be married when Bill received orders to be transferred back to the States in two weeks. Annie's parents suggested Bill take a week's leave to visit her relatives in Cologne that Bill hadn't met.

They went to Celle on a motorcycle with a side-car. Annie in the side car, her father (Pappa) driving and Bill behind him. A mechanical breakdown occurred and they got off the Autobahn well beyond the stone posts marking the limits of the emergency lane. Bill and Pappa were checking the motorcycle and Annie was lying on the grass about ten feet away, wrapped in a raincoat, when suddenly a section of the stone post that marked the emergency lane flew between Bill and Pappa. They looked to where Annie had been but she wasn't there! She was lying in the outside lane of the Autobahn, on her back and still wrapped in Bill's raincoat but her right leg was bent at a strange angle. At a local hospital, it was determined that about three inches above her knee, almost two inches of her thigh bone was crushed. The doctor said Annie would probably lose her leg as the hospital didn't have the proper medication and equipment to insert a metal brace to replace the missing portion of the bone. The doctor said there was a possibility she might grow new bone from both sides but didn't give it much hope. A British military unit stationed in town and a Company Sergeant Major insisted Bill stay with his family until he had to return to Celle. The hospital had a one-hour visiting period twice a day but Bill stayed with her all day, until his leave was up.

The final determining cause of the accident was a truck carrying 30 foot long rough-cut timber fastened to the trailer by two large chains at each end of the timber. As the truck came abreast of the accident location, the rear chain broke permitting the load to pivot and one of the planks struck Annie's leg, and since she was wrapped up in Bill's raincoat, pulled her and the raincoat into the road. It was felt that had it not been for the raincoat Annie's leg might have been torn off.

Bill returned to the States in August 1949 for an assignment at Chanute Air Force Base, Illinois. He and Annie exchanged letters and continued to make plans for their wedding. Annie wrote several letters asking Bill to forget her. She also wrote to Bill's mother asking her to discourage Bill as she felt Bill wouldn't want a wife with one leg. Bill's mother knew how much Bill loved her and told Annie even if needed there were artificial limbs available. In the latter part of October 1949, Annie's doctor put a body cast from her chest downward, including both legs, and had her go home.

Bill had a difficult time obtaining a 30-day leave to return to Germany to marry Annie. The personnel officer seemed to realize Bill really wanted to marry Annie and granted him a 30-day leave on the 20th of December. Military stipulations were placed on the leave which due to Bill's extensive research before leaving made him able to overcome in Germany.

Bill's reunion with Annie was wonderful. She was lying on the couch in a full body cast but as far as he was concerned the cast didn't exist. They couldn't get enough of just looking at one another. It was daybreak before Bill went upstairs to bed.

After spending Christmas together, Bill returned to Wiesbaden and Frankfurt several times to pick up forms required for marriage. The American medical authorities in Frankfurt at first insisted Annie had to go to them for the premarital physical. Bill showed them that the Air Force and Army regulations stated any Allied Medics Officer could perform the examination. Bill asked the Chief Medical Officer in the British armored unit stationed in Celle if he would be willing to give them a physical. The Officer answered in the affirmative. They could not have gotten married without the outstanding help given by the British Army unit.

Bill returned the completed paper work to Wiesbaden and received permission to marry. He thought nothing could stop them now. Time was running out, his leave would end in only a few more days, and arrangements still had to be made with the local authorities for the required civil wedding. The Clerk-of-Courts in City Hall said no exceptions could be made; they would have to go to City Hall to be married. It was impossible to bring Annie to City Hall as there was a thick layer of snow on the ground. Plans that had been made for a wedding reception the day before Bill was to leave were changed to a "Going Away" party.

The guests who had been invited to the wedding reception were now there for the newly named party. Just before the party was about to begin, there was a knock on the door. Pappa opened the door and there stood the Clerk-of-Courts with an interpreter and all the papers in German and English. He offered no explanation for bending the rule. He married Bill and Annie, who was in a full-body cast, reclining on the daybed with Bill standing beside her holding her hand.

This 18th of January, 1950 turned out to be a wonderful day. On this day they were officially married meeting the requirements of the law in Germany. Their church wedding would have to take place months later in the United States.

Bill left for the States the next day and wrote to Annie several times a week. She told him she was fitted with a "walking cast" and was learning to walk again. She had not been on her feet for almost seven months and had to undergo intensive and painful physical therapy to return motion to her knees. She told Bill she would bear the pain as she wanted to walk into his arms when she arrives in the States.

Bill, his mother, brother and sister-in-law drove to La Guardia Airport, New York and on the Fourth of July, 1950, Annie walked into Bill's arms!

Bill warned Annie that he was concerned about his grandfather who was against his marriage and had asked if Bill couldn't find a "nice Slovak or Hungarian girl." Even, as a last resort, an American girl who would be better than a German girl.

Annie was actually trembling at the thought of meeting Bill's grandfather. As they were climbing the steps to the porch, the screen door opened and there stood Bill's grandfather, a burly, white-haired man, a little over six feet and weighing about 250 pounds. Compared to Annie who was slender, with dark almost black hair, barely five feet tall and weighing about 96 pounds, he was a giant! Bill's grandfather looked at Annie, smiled, and greeting her in German scooped her up in his arms, kissed her and physically carried her into the house. They immediately became the best of friends and he became her ally forever.

Bill and Annie had a church wedding on July 15, 1950 in Youngstown, Ohio.

Several years after Bill and Annie settled down in Illinois, they arranged to have her father, mother and brother come to the United States as permanent immigrants. Both parents died of natural causes and are buried in Illinois.

It was found—probably due to the brutal treatment Annie received in the concentration camps—she couldn't have children. They adopted two children, one in Illinois and the second at Rhein-Main Air Base, Frankfurt, Germany. Both have done extremely well in school, are both PhDs and very successful in their chosen fields.

Annie single-handedly raised both boys while Bill was away on various assignments, including being sent to Viet Nam twice. He retired from the Air Force after 30 years of service and decided to make Texas their home.

Annie and Bill had 37 wonderful years together. After several years of serious illnesses and several major surgeries, Annie died of cancer on the last day of 1986.

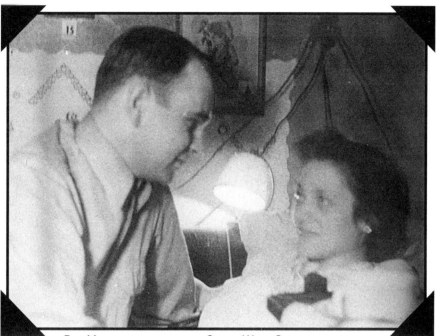

BILL MICHAELS RETURNED TO CELLE, WEST GERMANY TO MARRY HIS FIANCÉE, ANNIE KIRSCHBAUM, DURING THE 1949 CHRISTMAS SEASON.

BILL MICHAELS WITH ANNIE'S FAMILY IN DECEMBER 1949. (L-R) MARIA (MOTHER), HUBERT, JR., FAMILY FRIEND, ANNIE, BILL AND ANNIE'S FATHER HUBERT, SR.

CHAPTER 5
Ellie & James Spatafora

JAMES (IN NEW AIR FORCE UNIFORM) AND ELLIE IN WINTER OF 1950 AFTER THEY WERE MARRIED. PHOTO TAKEN IN DINGOLFING, BAVARIA WHILE VISITING ELLIE'S MOTHER.

Questions to and answers from:
Mr. James Spatafora

In finding the love of his life, James Spatafora said, "In a crazy way I thank the USSR, because if they had not 'blockaded' Berlin, I would not have gone to Germany and met 'Ellie.'" Jim often uses the phrase "we are one" when referring to his love Ellie.

When and where were you born?
    May 19, 1929, New York City (Manhattan), New York.

Were you raised on a farm, in a village, city, suburbs, etc.?
City.

How many were in your family and composition of same?
Five: Mother, father, two sisters, and myself.

Was your family structured in a strict, moderate or loose manner?
Moderate.

What amount of formal education did you acquire?
Four years of college; no degree.

How, generally speaking, did all or any particular part of the above affect your adult attitude prior to and during your Berlin Airlift assignment?
All.

When and what circumstance led you to become a member of the military?
Draft was on. I did not wish to be drafted, so I enlisted.

What were the factors that led to your Berlin Airlift assignment?
Volunteered to go to Germany.

What was your rank and duties?
Private First Class (PFC), P-51 Hydraulic Specialist.

What were the living conditions at your base?
Terrible at Rhein/Main.

What were the living conditions of the German people at the time?

Very bad for most Germans.

Describe your inner feelings towards the German people you encountered at the time.

No different, felt sorry at what a stupid war can do.

It has been said Germans were starving in some areas while the military poured gasoline on many loaves of bread and burned them because they were stale. Did anything of this nature occur where you were assigned? If it did, what feelings did you have?

Never, we supported three orphanages with food from the mess hall.

What was the general attitude of the American military and German people towards one another when you were first assigned there? If tense when did it change, if it did, and what were some indications you noticed?

Tense sometimes, deadly; and members of the military didn't dare go out alone for fear of having their throats slit and being thrown in the river. But from July 1948 to December 1948, a miracle took place. The dramatic change occurred when they saw what we were doing to keep them free…even losing our lives. The base would get calls from families who had very little for themselves asking if any member of the military would like to have a German meal in their home.

When did you first see or become aware of your wife-to-be?

September 1949.

What was your first impression when you saw her?
　　Became very fond of her.

When did you begin to realize you were falling in love?
　　November 1949.

What were some of the outstanding highlights of your courtship: where did you meet, how did you meet (was it difficult to get passes from the base), where did you go, was there any negative reaction from Germans seeing the two of you together?
　　Introduced by a mutual friend, Staff Sergeant, Glen Dotson.

When and where did you propose marriage? Did she accept your proposal at the time? What was your reaction?

　　December 1949. Ellie was a bit hesitant at first.

What were the reactions of your military friends when realizing you had fallen in love and intended to marry a local German lady?
　　Not favorable.

What were the reactions of her parents, relatives and friends upon learning she was in love and accepted your proposal of marriage?
　　Resigned.

What were the official requirements for marriage? Were obstacles put in your way and if so, why? How long did it take before you were officially married?

Many, many bureaucratic obstacles over one year for two of four weddings. *(See "Addendum" for an elaboration of "four" weddings.)*

Where were you married? Describe such things as the setting and who attended?

Rhein/Main Air Force Base, Standisamt, State Department and Edwards Air Force Base.

What adjustments were made in performing your military obligations as a married man?

I now had two responsibilities.

When and where did you return to the States? Was it direct from your Berlin Airlift assignment or from additional foreign service elsewhere?

I stayed after the Berlin Airlift until January 3, 1952.

How did you help your bride adjust to being in the US? Did she speak English?

She spoke little English–soap operas helped.

Were relatives and neighbors friendly to her and did they go out of their way to make her feel welcome? Did anyone ever give her a difficult time?

Some relatives were friendly, most were not.

Describe how through the years your bride's adjustment developed.

Great, she was involved and still is in many activities.

Do you have children? If so give an indepth elaboration.

One daughter Jacqueline and two sons, Ronni and Jeffrey.

Has your wife returned to Germany to visit her relatives, either alone, or with you and/or with your children? In turn have her relatives been here?

Many times with and without me. Yes!

Why are you so proud and happy that the love of your life became your wife?

She would be the only one! We are equals.

ADDENDUM: As told by James Spatafora

I was born on 19 May 1929 in Manhattan (New York City). My mother was a widow until she remarried some years later. Eventually I had one brother and two sisters, I was raised mostly by my mother's father (my grandfather) who among many successful careers was at one time a New York City Police Detective; he was firm but always fair. I loved and respected him at all times. My family was generally moderate.

My early years were uneventful. Upon graduating junior high school, I took an entrance exam to enter the most prestigious and oldest aviation high school in the US, the Manhattan High School of Aviation (SAT) which was located on 63rd and 64th Streets in Manhattan. I studied all facets of civil aviation and shortly after graduating, I enlisted in the United States Army Air Force. After basic training, I was sent to Keesler Field, Mississippi to become an Army Air Force Aircraft Mechanic.

Then I was sent to the P-51 Specialist School and then to Kearney Air Field, Nebraska to the P-51 squadron. I was put in the hydraulic shop and reclassified as a P-51 hydraulic specialist. While at Kearney, the Russians blockaded Berlin for the second time and volunteers were called to go to Germany and participate in what was to become the "Berlin Airlift."

I had never ever seen a C-54 Hydraulic System and all of a sudden I was the one and only C-54 Hydraulic Specialist at Rhein/Main Air Base. I worked my tail off; I had no one to teach me the C-54 hydraulic systems. I would sometimes work two to three days without sleep and maybe eat one meal a day in the mess hall, the rest of the time called for plenty of coffee and cigarettes. Eventually, as I worked faster, I had time to study and then taught photography. I also studied the Russian language all during my very few "off duty" hours. I was still a Private First Class when the "Lift" ended. I was promoted to Corporal in September 1949, and shortly after that a friend Staff/Sergeant Glenn Dotson from Texas, introduced me to my "Bride" of the past 48 years as of Christmas Eve of 1998.

Ellie worked in a dry cleaning store near the Haupbahnhop in Frankfurt. I used to take my laundry and uniforms to be dry cleaned once a week to the store she worked in. We started dating, and on the "first" date we were supposed to see a movie at the British movie theater in Frankfurt. I waited for hours for her to show up, but she had to work late and I didn't know why she had not arrived at the theater on time. I thought maybe she changed her mind about going to a movie with a "GI" but waited, and eventually she got to the theater. I'm glad I waited or our lives could have been completely different.

At home I was not taught to "hate" so I could not hate the Germans or the Russians or Cubans or even the Vietnamese years later. What pleased me most of all about "Ellie" was she would not take anything from me; no stockings, no candy bars, no cigarettes, she would only accept soap which was hard to get in Germany at that time. I could get all I wanted at the Post Exchange (PX) on Rhein/Main Air Base.

In December 1949, I asked Ellie to marry me. At first she seemed reluctant. When she agreed, we decided to visit her mother, father, two brothers and her younger sister who lived in a farm house in a little village northeast of Munich (Dingolfing) home of the BMW for the past 45 years.

It was a cold Bavarian night when we arrived to meet her family. They came to meet us at the little train station. Her older brother was in the German Army (also a Corporal). When her brother's eyes met mine, there was a moment of silent staring and then we both laughed and had a snow ball fight. I'm sure Ellie was very worried that her family, especially her older brother would not accept me into the family as her husband. There was an instant bond between her brother and me which only soldiers share and understand regardless of which army they were in during the war. War is stupid and no one hates war more than a sane soldier or sailor. I was too young to be "drafted" but I wanted some control over my destiny, which is why I "enlisted" and why I "volunteered" to go to Germany to participate in the Berlin Airlift.

In a crazy sort of way I thank the USSR because if they had not "blockaded" Berlin I would not have gone to Germany and met "Ellie." Conditions in Germany were "bad" for everybody…shortages of food and other necessities for living, not only for the Germans and refugees but for everyone. The winter of 1948 to 1949 was the worst winter in some 80 years. We flew to Berlin where even the birds were "walking" and that is no myth or joke, it's the truth! Mud was everywhere on the Rhein/Main Air Base. The cold crystallizing fog went right through your clothing no matter how much clothing you were wearing. When I flew to Berlin that winter I wore my summer underwear. Although I later wore my winter underwear, summer khaki uniform, work fatigues, flying suit, sheep skin trousers, and jacket, I was still cold almost all of the time.

I loved my job and the people I worked with—both the Germans and Americans. "It was the best and the worst of times for humanity," to quote another author. When I first arrived in Germany, there was understandably, a lot of hatred for the Americans. One did not go to the German cities alone. We usually went to Frankfurt in groups of two's or three's— never alone for fear you would wind up in the Maine River face down with your throat cut.

From July to December 1948 I saw a miracle take place. We Americans, who were so hated in July, started to die during the "Lift." We died in our aircraft crashes; we died in ground accidents and from other causes. Our sacrifices coupled with the horror stories told by the refugees who were escaping from East Germany, Poland, Hungary and other East Bloc Countries of how they were treated by the Russians and the Police and Armies of the Communist Countries had such an affect on Germans in the French, British and American Zones of Occupation. I remember it very clearly as if it was just yesterday...German families who did not have enough food to feed themselves were contacting the Chaplains on Rhein/Maine Air Base and other places asking the Chaplains if they knew of any American GI's who would like to eat Christmas dinner in their German homes instead of the mess hall.

What a tremendous change in the attitude of some of the German people in just six months. We did other humanitarian acts not connected with the Berlin Airlift; when we went to eat in the mess hall we would take more food than we planned on eating. We would eat what we wanted from one side of the tray and put untouched food on the other end of the tray. When we went to empty the trays after we finished eating, we would carefully separate the untouched food and put it in separate containers. Meat in one container, bread in another, potatoes in another, etc. The clean untouched food was collected by nuns from three orphanages in and around Frankfurt to feed themselves and the orphans. You see we could not give the food to the orphanages but we found a way to get around the rules by giving them *"clean garbage"* which was exactly what we GI's were eating in the mess hall.

Back to Ellie. Most of my comrades, family and especially the military were against fraternization and marriages between GI's and Germans. Ellie stood with me together and faced an unbelievable amount of bureaucratic paperwork and harassment. It seemed as if the whole world was against our marrying; in the end we won. We were married in a German Civil Ceremony by the Oberburgermeister Kolb of Frankfurt, the American Civil Authorities and finally by the Military Protestant Chaplain Lindemann. The reason for so many ceremonies was because the military did not recognize the American or German Civil Authorities. The German did not recognize the American Civil or Military authorities, etc.

Ellie who was Lutheran could not be married in a Catholic ceremony. It was not until ten years later while we were stationed at Edwards Air Force Base, California (from May 1956 to January 1963) that Father (Chaplain) McDonald wrote the military ordinariate (Chief of Chaplains) for all of the Armed Forces Cardinal Spellman stating that I had 12 years in the Air Force, a going career, a wife since December 1949, three children...the third born at Edwards Air Force Base. I had been through every rank from Private to First Lieutenant and asked he please give us permission to marry in the Catholic Church.

Well, Father McDonald was transferred to Alaska and Father Klaric was assigned to take Father McDonald's place. In December 1959, Cardinal Spellman wrote to Father Klaric, and in so many words told Father Klaric that he, Cardinal Spellman, as a Tenth Anniversary present to Ellie and me would allow us to be married in the Catholic Church on base providing we got married on the same hour of the day we were originally married. We finally married for the fourth time the afternoon of 24 December, 1959 exactly on our tenth anniversary. Our three children attended the wedding along with some close friends.

Ellie & James Spatafora (123)

Questions to and answers from:
Mrs. Ellie Spatafora

James Spatafora said, "Ellie had a very difficult time answering questions since it not only brought back good memories but also some very bad ones— especially during the war years. She had nightmares for many years after we married; they have gradually faded with time."

When were you born?
June 1, 1927.

Were you raised on a farm, in a village, etc.?
A village in East Prussia.

How many were in your family and composition of same?
Six: Mother, father, sister and two brothers.

Was your family structured in a strict, moderate or loose manner?
Mother strict, father moderate.

What amount of formal education did you acquire?
Eight years of grade school and three years of business school.

What was the economical and political atmosphere in Germany and how did it affect your immediate family and others both near and far?
Too busy with school to think about and living in the country.

How, generally speaking, did all or any particular part of the above

affect your adult attitude prior to, during, and immediately following the war's end?

I was a school girl and lost everything.

When did you and others begin to feel Germany would be in war? Was this looked upon with favor and/or fear?

We were on the border of Poland and saw all the German troops.

Did the war's early victories cause a feeling of euphoria - that Germany was so powerful no country on earth could stop it?

I had a feeling of fear.

What were some of your home front war time activities in the early stages of the war?

We were living in a small village and busy trying to make a living.

What was the general feeling when Germany opened the Russian front? How did this affect your home front activities?

My mother and father came from Russia and knew we would never make it.

Did bombing or fighting take place where you lived? If so, to what extent?

We left my house 1944 and saw, Dresden, Czechoslovakia, Austria and the Russians.

(See addendum for additional information.)

What effect did the war have on everyday living, e.g., shortages, attitude, travel, etc.?

Living in the country we had more to eat because we lived off the land.

When and how did your hear of the Japanese attack at Pearl Harbor and the US's entry into World War II?

On the radio.

What were the thoughts and impact of Germans to the US's entry into the war?

I was a child.

What was the general opinion of Germans to the US prior to World War II?

Good, my father had his sister in America since 1933.

As the war progressed what was the general opinion of German civilians to the American military who were fighting the German Military? Also, how did German civilians feel the American military, involved in combat, would treat them at this time?

We lived on the run from the missions and thought the Americans were better.

Was the Russian military anywhere near your home area?

Yes, we were in Austria under Russian occupation.

**As the war progressed what was the general opinion of Germans civilians to the Russian military who were fighting the German military? Also, how did Germans civilians feel the Russian military, involved in combat, would treat them at this time?

It was a nightmare!

Did your area receive much war damage? Explain the extent to people and property.

My home was not destroyed. It is farm country.

When did it seem assured Germany would lose the war? What were the outstanding fears of the apparent loss?

I saw three 15-year old boys killed in the town by Germans in 1944.

What was the reaction when the war ended and Germany lost? Was there general dissension or cooperation among your neighbors regarding the loss at this time?

My family lost everything and my father and brother were soldiers.

What were the conditions in your area when the war ended? Were there shortages of vital needs? What were the outstanding fears of the apparent loss?

We lost everything and had to live on very little.

What was the feeling toward the American military when the war ended and they occupied the area-if they did? Were the occupiers friendly and considerate or were they to be feared?

Americans were good to us. My dad's sister helped from America.

What were some of the outstanding things the American military

occupiers might have done that had you appreciate them or vice-versa, fear them?

> We did get some food and a place to live when we came to the US zone.

Describe the tension that both sides probably had towards each other and how this tension in time eased. What factors led to the easing of tension? Did the Americans help the local economy by making purchases of items or assorted types of services?

> *(See "Addendum" for additional information.)*

When did you first see or become aware of your husband-to-be?

> He came to the store where I worked.

What was your first impression when you saw him?

> He was quiet.

When did you begin to realize you were falling in love?

> Not too long after we met.

What were some of the outstanding highlights of your being courted: where did you meet, how did you meet, were you working at the time, and where did you go?

> We met in the dry cleaning store. We had little money. We had a few places we loved and enjoyed.

When and where did you receive a proposal of marriage? Did you

accept the proposal at the time? How did you feel—what was your reaction?

I accepted his proposal in Frankfurt. It was difficult to leave my family.

What were the reactions of your parents, relatives and friends upon learning you were in love with an American military man and accepted his proposal of marriage?

My father and mother were happy for me, but they knew I would leave for America—we were a close family.

What were the official requirements for marriage? Do you feel obstacles were put in the way and if so, why? How long did it take before your were officially married?

At the time we got married the obstacles were strict. They did not look with favor on German women going to the US. We got married on the 24th of December of 1949.

Where were you married? Describe such things as the setting and those in attendance.

We got married in Rhein Main Chapel. Two friends were with us.

If married in Germany what adjustments did you have to make to be with your husband? Where did you live, etc.

We lived in Frankfurt at first, then Kelsterbach and elsewhere.

Where, when, and how did you go to the States?

I left for the US on a boat from Holland in April 1952.

Did you speak English when you arrived? How were you treated and how were you helped to adjust to the new country? Did your husband's relatives and friends go out of their way to be of help and make you feel welcome?

I spoke little English. My husband's relatives were not too kind. Only one aunt was friendly, making up for all of them.

Describe how through the years your adjustment developed.

I adapted fast in the US. We moved a lot in the Air Force.

Do you have children? If so give an indepth elaboration regarding their births, upbringing and present status.

We have three children. One in California, one in Texas and one in New Mexico. They are all doing well.

Have you ever returned to Germany to visit your relatives? If so, were your husband and children with you? In turn have your relatives visited you in the States?

We go to Germany often. My family have all been here and loved it very much.

Why are you so proud and happy that the love of your life became your husband?

We were in the US Air Force 29 years and have seen a lot. We have had good and bad times. We retired and now are busy with many things.

ADDENDUM: "Ellie" – As told by James Spatafora

I hope Ellie will not have a recurrence of nightmares as a result of this survey. When we first met she was frightened of the times. After the war years, she was working very hard and was "refugee status" according to the then German authorities in power at the time. Her family was scattered during the war as were so many other families. She worked for a short time in a circus as a trapeze artist on the "high wire" and then for an alcoholic "knife thrower"—she was the target. He finally pinned her skirt to the backboard with one of the knives just to "prove" how good he was with the knives. Ellie's father made her quit the circus.

That is when she started working at the dry cleaning store. She did work a while in a US Army mess hall after they got out of the detention camps immediately after the war. She used to bring home coffee grounds and anything else the Army threw away. She was about 100 miles away when the Allies were bombing Dresden. She still remembers how the ground shook like an earthquake even though she was 100 miles away. During the war when she went to visit her brother, Richard, who was stationed in Berlin as a Corporal Tank Driver, she spent almost all of the time in bomb shelters since this was about the time Allies were bombing Berlin day and night.

I did my best to make memories of her war experiences lessen since I knew I could never make her forget completely what she had endured along with so many others of so many nationalities. We did not have much money (I only made about $34 a month) so we did things we could afford; like take long walks along the river in Frankfurt or go to a movie or just ride around in the street cars for what seemed like hours.

A few months after we were married she got a bad kidney infection. She could not be treated by the military doctors since she was not "American." We had no other medical benefits, so they finally let her in at the German hospital in Langen. She suffered greatly for some seven weeks. There were no doctors in that hospital, just "Nuns." I tried to visit her every night. Nobody would give a GI like me a ride especially at night, so I would walk nine miles one way to the hospital and go from Rhein/Main Air Base where I worked on the flight line to Mittledich to Sprendlinger to Buschlag and to Langen. Remember, it was February 1950 and it was so very cold.

By the time I got to the hospital it was two to three hours after I left the base and it was after visiting hours. The Nuns knew what my life was like and felt sorry. I guess, because when I rattled the chain of the iron gates, one of the Nuns would come and unchain the gates, I would give her a pack of cigarettes. She would then escort me to Ellie's bedside and let me stay for 15 minutes then escort me to the gate and lock the gate after I left. I would then walk back another nine miles.

It would be about midnight before I got home, and then I hitchhiked to work next morning at Rhein/Main Air Base. While she was ill at the beginning, she could not keep anything down in her stomach, not even water. The Nuns found out Ellie would not throw up strawberries so to keep her from dehydrating I found sources in Sprendling where they were growing strawberries in hot houses in that winter of 1950. I "black-marketed" my whole "soul" to get those strawberries to her as often as I could until she could drink water and hold down some foods and start to get some strength back. When she finally got out of the hospital, I was almost ready to collapse; but I never stopped loving her and would do it again if I had to. I don't think I will ever forget, and I hope she never remembers.

Addendum II: - "Ellie" As told by James Spatafora.

Ellie was living in that part of Germany which was called "East Prussia," even in those early days she knew Germany was at war but what does that mean to a 12-year-old? The war was almost over when she was 17 years old and with her mother, younger brother and sister virtually "walked" from East Prussia to Austria. She realized Germany was losing the war when she worked in the German parachute factory near Dresden and experienced the constant day and nighttime bombing of Dresden. She still had nightmares 15 years later. She didn't wake up screaming like you see in the movies, but she did wake up crying. Gradually over the years it subsided, but I still try to avoid any mention of war and her experiences.

While Ellie and I are both of European stock, the German and American cultures have significant differences. We Americans are "democratic" and definitely "march to a different drummer." "The Germans were more methodical, regimented with the central government mindset." You did not question the Hitler government. When you are raised that way, thinking like an American is inconceivable. Even before we met, she had to start recognizing the differences in our two cultures and start adapting to our American ways. Bear in mind she was now 21, much of her life had been under Hitler, her country fought and lost a world war during her teenage years and is "conquered" by these "American, British, Russians and French invaders." One can only imagine how we would feel.

Gradually—especially after the *Berlin Airlift* started—she (along with most Germans) started to see the Americans in a different light. Yes, we still had the drunks, the loud mouths, the rapists—but for the most part,

Americans were not the monsters which the Germans thought during and immediately after the war. The Americans were quickly differentiated from the Russians and how they treated the Germans. To the Germans, despite their faults and "boorish" behavior the Americans were "Saints" when compared to the way the Russians treated Germans in East Berlin and East Germany.

She saw that most of the American "occupiers" were young soldiers, airmen who probably didn't want to be there in the first place but were making the best of it. She may not have fully realized the money these GI's were pumping into the German economy—at least not at the beginning, but my going to the dry cleaning store along with so many other GI's and the coo-coo clocks we bought and so many other goods and services we paid for made some Germans "millionaires." We GI's didn't buy just beer and schnapps and sexual favors (for want of a better phrase). Add to this the lives we lost during the lift were factors that ease the strained relationship.

You have no idea how Ellie and I struggled financially, socially, culturally, etc., especially the first few years of our marriage. We raised a family of four on $34 a month. When 19, I returned to the United States on January 3, 1952; I left with $3 in my pocket. I left Ellie about $50 which was all we had.

She finally arrived in the United States four months later. Because of a temporary quirk in US Immigration Law, I could not sponsor my wife and children to the United States, but my 18-month-old daughter—an American citizen (actually she had dual citizenship since she was born in Germany)—sponsored her mother (Ellie) and her six-month-old brother on her (Jacqueline's) American passport.

I flew from San Antonio, Texas during the night to New York and then went by ferry to New Jersey to meet Ellie and the kids. I stood there while everyone got off the ship; no Ellie, no kids. I found the ship's purser and asked what happened to my family. He checked the ship's manifest and showed me where Ellie and the kids got off in Halifax, Newfoundland. Now I was really angry. Ellie spoke very little English and was even less able to read English. What was I going to do about me in New Jersey and my family in Newfoundland?

Just about when I was ready to give up, I saw Ellie and the kids coming down the gangplank. The rest is history!

JAMES AND ELLIE AT THE 1996 BERLIN AIRLIFT VETERANS ASSOCIATION REUNION DINNER IN DAYTON, OHIO.

(L-R) ELLIE'S SISTER-IN-LAW RIA, ELLIE'S OLDER BROTHER, RICHARD, AND ELLIE. RICHARD LIVED THREE KILOMETERS FROM THEIR PARENTS IN A TOWN CALLED, STEINBERG, BAVARIA.

CHAPTER 6
Hedda & Forrest E. Ott

FORREST AND HEDDA WEDDING PHOTO, DECEMBER 13, 1950 AT COLUMBIA HOUSE (OFFICER'S CLUB) IN TEMPELHOF AIRPORT.

Questions to and answers from:
Mr. Forrest E. Ott

"After being back in the USA for about eight months or so, I decided to go back to Germany as a civilian and marry her. I wrote her that I was coming and that I would like to marry her if she would have me."

When and where were you born?

May 10, 1921 in Wergeland Township, Central Western Minnesota.

Were you raised on a farm, in a village, city, suburbs, etc.?
On a farm

How many were in your family and composition of same?
Total of five, Mother, father and two sisters.

Was your family structured in a strict, moderate or loose manner?
Quite a strict manner.

What amount of formal education did you acquire?
Three years of college, majored in Physics and Math.

How, generally speaking, did all or any particular part of the above affect your adult attitude prior to and during your Berlin Airlift assignment?
My father was of German descent, therefore I felt a special closeness to the German people. My grandfather was a German immigrant.

When and what circumstances led you to become a member of the military?
I was flying as a civilian in the Army Air Corps Reserve and was called to active duty in 1943. Was sent to aviation cadet flying school to train as a military pilot.

What were the factors that led to your Berlin Airlift assignment?
After the war ended, I went to Air Route Traffic Control School, graduating in December, 1945. Was transferred to Frankfurt in early 1946 as Air Traffic Controller. Then, in April, 1948 was transferred to Berlin Air

Safety Center located in the Allied Control Authority Building in Berlin, to control air traffic in and out of Berlin. This was before the Airlift started.

What was your rank and duties?

First Lieutenant; Controlled air traffic in and out of Berlin. Also flew 110 missions in the Airlift during the period that I was "off duty" as an Air Traffic Controller.

What were the living conditions at your base?

Was based at Tempelhof Air Base. Conditions were very good for us.

What were the living conditions of the German people at the time?

The German people did not really have enough to eat, that is; the people who lived in Berlin. Also, all during the winter of 48-49, they were limited to two hours of electricity per day. The two hours might be in the middle of the night. When it came on, they would get up and cook, or wash clothes, or heat apartments or whatever they had to do. Coal for heating homes was almost impossible for them to obtain.

Describe your inner feelings towards the German people you encountered at the time.

Many Americans felt sorry for the German people and would give German friends food items or items of clothing occasionally, especially during the Airlift. Germans would sell jewelry, cameras, beer steins etc., to Americans for American cigarettes, which they would in turn trade for black market food, clothes, etc. I personally felt sorry for the German people, and often wondered how they could ever allow someone like Hitler to control them as he did.

It has been said Germans were starving in some areas while the military poured gasoline on many loaves of bread and burned them because they were stale. Did anything of this nature occur where you were assigned? If it did, what feelings did you have?

I was not aware of this ever happening.

What was the general attitude of the American military and German people towards one another when you were first assigned there? If tense when did it change, if it did, and what were some indications you noticed?

Upon arrival in early 1946, there was some lingering hatred between Germans and Occupation troops. We carried side arms if we went uptown. But this hatred disappeared by the end of 1946. The hatred was worse in Bavaria. By 1947, they were much friendlier. Time has a way of healing animosities.

When did you first see or become aware of your wife-to-be?

She was working as a cashier at the Officer's Mess at Tempelhof AFB in early Fall of 1948.

What was your first impression when you saw her?

She was a cute little thing and spoke excellent English.

When did you begin to realize you were falling in love?

When I started feeling sorry for her and her living conditions.

What were some of the outstanding highlights of your courtship:

where did you meet, how did you meet (was it difficult to get passes from the base), where did you go, was there any negative reaction from Germans seeing the two of you together?

Hedda was working temporarily as a cashier at the Templehof Officer's Mess, the Columbia House, when I first met her. This was in May or early June, shortly before the airlift started. I though she was very pretty, had a nice smile, and spoke good English. So, after seeing her several times at the mess, I got up enough courage to ask her out one evening after she got off from work. I had a little Fiat car and we drove to a German club for a couple of drinks and some dancing. I then drove her home where she lived with her mother, and two nieces. I had a sailing boat down on Lake Wannsee that I had leased from Special Services and we made a date to go sailing the next Saturday or Sunday. She enjoyed sailing. We went sailing nearly every week-end for the rest of the summer.

Most of the highlights of our courtship were sailing on the boat and going to the Sailing Club in the evening. We would also go to the Army club occasionally which was down by Headquarters. As an employee of the U.S. Air Force at Tempelhof, she had a permanent pass to the air base. There were not many German places to go to while the airlift was in progress. I was not allowed to bring her to the Officer's Club at Tempelhof as my guest since she was an employee there. I leased a different boat (a racing sloop) the next year, also on Lake Wannsee. I joined the American Yachting Association that year, and we participated in races nearly every week end. We even won a couple of racing prizes. I had a red long-haired Dachshund that love to go sailing with us. Hedda would keep her for me, since I could not have her in the Officer's billets at the Columbia House.

We did not receive any negative reaction from the German people from seeing the two of us together. The only negative reaction we received was from the higher ranking officers about our coming together into the Tempelhof Officer's Club

I was rotated back to the States in November, 1949. I returned to Berlin in December, 1950 as a tourist, and Hedda and I were married on December 13 at the Tempelhof Standesamt. Our wedding reception was at the Columbia House.

When and where did you propose marriage? Did she accept your proposal at the time? What was your reaction?

After being back in the USA for about eight months or so, I decided to go back to Germany as a civilian and marry her. I wrote to tell her that I was coming and that I would like to marry her if she would have me.

What were the reactions of your military friends when realizing you had fallen in love and intended to marry a local German lady?

I did not have any military friends at this time as I was a civilian in the USA (Texas).

What was the reaction of her parents, relatives and friends upon learning she was in love and accepted your proposal of marriage?

Her parents, sisters, and friends were happy for her, that I was coming back to marry her.

What were the official requirements for marriage? Were obstacles put in your way and if so, why? How long did it take before you

were officially married?

Since I was a civilian, all we needed to marry was a German marriage license. We were married December 13, 1950. This was about a week after my arrival over there.

Where were you married? Describe such things as the setting and who attended?

We were married in the Zehlendorf Standesamt. Her family and several of my military friends who were still stationed in Berlin attended the ceremony. We had a reception afterward at the Tempelhof AFB Officers Club, where I had been a member when I was stationed there.

What adjustments were made in performing your military obligations as a married man?

None were necessary. I did not return to active duty till May, 1951.

When and where did you return to the States? Was it direct from your Berlin Airlift assignment or from additional foreign service elsewhere?

I had to return to the States about a week after we were married. Hedda had to obtain an immigration visa which took about six months to get. She finally arrived in Dallas, Texas in June of 1951. By this time, I had been called back to active duty in the US Air Force.

How did you help your bride adjust to being in the US? Did she speak English?

She did not have any problem adjusting to life in the US, since she had lived in Montreal, Canada for ten years as a young girl in school, and spoke excellent English.

Were relatives and neighbors friendly to her and did they go out of their way to make her feel welcome? Did anyone ever give her a difficult time?

Relatives and friend were friendly to her. No one ever gave her a difficult time.

Describe how through the years your bride's adjustment developed.

Her adjustment developed rapidly since she had such a wonderful command of the English language. She adapted to the life as wife of an Air Force Officer rapidly.

In January of 1953, I was transferred to a new assignment in Okinawa. Arrangements were made for her to live with her sister in Pennsylvania until she could come to Okinawa. Her sister had married a US Army Sergeant and they were living there. Hedda had immediately applied for US Citizenship when we found out that I was going back overseas. She was sworn in as a Citizen of the United States about the first of July 1953. She got orders to join me in Okinawa shortly thereafter, arriving around the 1st of September.

Do you have children? If so give an indepth elaboration.

We have had four children - three girls and 1 boy. They are as follows:

Beatrice, Age 43, married, lives in Baton Rouge, Louisiana. She is a

Hedda & Forrest E. Ott (145)

Ph D., and a Vice-President of South Eastern Louisiana University. She has one son who will graduate from LSU on August 1st.

Patricia, Age 41, married to Donald Wessinge, Shipping Manager for Export-Import Company and a Girl Scout Troop leader.

Duane - Age 40, has a Master's degree in Computer Science. He is a Software Engineer for Compu Serve in the Headquarters in Columbus, Ohio. He is married, but has no children.

Marilyn, Age 38, is our youngest. She is a Doctor, a Captain in the Air Force Medical Service. She is married to Lt. Col. Ricardo Mora, a US Air Force Doctor. She has two children, girl 15 and boy 13.

Has your wife returned to Germany to visit her relatives, either alone, or with you and/or with your children? In turn have her relatives been here?

She and I have both been back for visits four different times. We plan to go again for the Berlin Airlift Reunion in 1999. She has very little family left in Germany. Hedda's mother emigrated to this country in 1955 and lived with us part time and with Hedda's sister part time. She passed away in 1981 and is buried in West Virginia. Hedda's sister lives in Savannah, Georgia and we see her occasionally.

Why are you so proud and happy that the love of your life became your wife?

We have had 46 good years together and have four lovely children and five beautiful grand-children.

Questions to and answers from:
Mrs. Hedda Ott

"In November, 1949 he had to return to the States...and then became a civilian. We exchanged a few letters, until the last one from him stated that it was all over which made me feel very sad. I heard nothing from him for over a year. Then one day a letter arrived saying he was coming back to Berlin to get married. I was so surprised (practically shocked) that I wasn't capable of telling him to stay where he was."

When and where you born?

1919 in Stuttgart, Germany.

Were you raised on a farm, in a village, etc.?

City

How many were in your family and composition of same?

Five: Father, mother and three girls.

Was your family structured in a strict, moderate or loose manner?

In a strict manner.

What amount of formal education did you acquire?

Four years of high school and two years of business college.

What was the economical and political atmosphere in Germany and how did it affect your immediate family and others both near and far?

Economical atmosphere was good, but the political was mixed with fear.

How, generally speaking, did all or any particular part of the above affect your adult attitude prior to, during, and immediately following the war's end?

Can't recall.

When did you and others begin to feel Germany would be in war? Was this looked upon with favor and/or fear?

Shortly before it started in September, 1939. It was looked upon with fear.

Did the war's early victories cause a feeling of euphoria that Germany was so powerful no country on earth could stop it?

Somewhat at the beginning.

What were some of your home front war time activities in the early stages of the war?

Member of the Red Cross assisting German soldiers in transit at train stations.

How long a period of time transpired before it was realized the war would take longer for Germany to win than expected?

Not until 1943 when the Americans entered the war.

What was the general feeling when Germany opened the Russian front? How did this affect your home front activities?

It wasn't too good. At the beginning not too much.

Did bombing or fighting take place where you lived? If so, to what extent?

Yes, we were bombed out totally four months before the war ended.

What effect did the war have on everyday living, e.g., shortages, attitude, travel, etc.?

There were shortages of just about everything, especially food. War caused my father to die of a heart attack. During World War II my parents lived in a small village about 50km from Berlin, here the film company he worked for, had moved cameras and other equipment. As the Russians were approaching in February 1945, the film equipment was moved into the bunkers the company had specially built in the woods. While carrying some of that to the shelters, he suffered a fatal heart attack. It was a terrible time for my mother and me.

At the beginning, the war had not had too much of an effect on every day living. We went on with our lives as usual. Later on ration cards were issued and food shortages, etc., became noticeable. It seemed as if we lived entirely on potatoes and cabbage, cooked as in many ways as one can possibly imagine. If one had enough money the grocer could be bribed into selling you something better from under the counter. Travel was still available up until 1943-44, travel on trains was uncomfortable and over crowded. The attitude of the people slowly declined as time went on.

When and how did you hear of the Japanese attack at Pearl Harbor and the US entry into World War II?

Had no knowledge of the Pearl Harbor attack.

What were the thoughts and impact of Germans to the US entry into the war?

That the war would last longer

What was the general opinion of Germans to the US prior to World War II?

There were a lot of mixed opinions.

As the war progressed what was the general opinion of German civilians to the American military who were fighting the German Military? Also, how did German civilians feel the American military, involved in combat, would treat them at this time?

In general the opinions of German civilians to the US was good!

Was the Russian military anywhere near your home area?

The Russians were the first to enter the village where we lived toward the end of the war.

As the war progressed what was the general opinion of Germans civilians to the Russian military who were fighting the German military? Also, how did German civilians feel the Russian military, involved in combat, would treat them at this time?

The Germans definitely preferred American occupation over the Russians.

Did your area receive much war damage? Explain the extent to people and property.

Ruins all over Berlin. Yes it was devastating for both people and property.

When did it seem assured Germany would lose the war? What were the outstanding fears of the apparent loss?

At the time both powers reached the Elbe.

What was the reaction when the war ended and Germany lost? Was there general dissension or cooperation among your neighbors regarding the loss at this time?

Utter dismay, but had to go on from there no matter what.

What were the conditions in your area when the war ended? Were there shortages of vital needs? What were the outstanding fears of the apparent loss?

Shortages of just everything and wide spread destruction.

What was the feeling towards the American military when the war ended and they occupied the area-if they did? Were the occupiers friendly and considerate or were they to be feared

Better the American occupation than the Russian. The American military was friendly.

What were some of the outstanding things the American military occupiers might have done that had you appreciate them or, vice-versa, fear them?

As I spoke fluent English, I found work at the Tempelhof Air Base for which I was very grateful.

Describe the tension that both sides probably had toward each other and how this tension in time eased. What factors led to the easing of tension? Did the Americans help the local economy by making purchases of items or assorted types of services?

I don't think there was much tension on either side. Helped out with some services.

When did you first see or become aware of your husband-to-be?

I knew who he was before he ever met me.

What was your first impression when you saw him?

That he was always in a hurry.

When did you begin to realize you were falling in love?

Probably when it was time for him to go back home.

What were some of the outstanding highlights of your being courted: where did you meet, how did you meet, were you working at the time, and where did you go?

There were really no highlights of a courtship. We met at Tempelhof Air Base where I worked. First as a receptionist at the Officers' BOQ, then at the Public Information Office. Intermittently I helped out as cashier at the Officers' Mess. That is when he asked me for a date (slightly inebriated). On weekends we usually went to the Army Officers' Club for dinner and sometimes dancing. We also sailed sometime on the Wanasee. The subject "marriage" was never discussed. In November, 1949 he had to return to the States through the RIF — and then became a civilian. We exchanged a few letters, until the last one from him stating that it was all over which made me very sad. I heard nothing from him again for over a year. Then one day a letter arrived saying that he was coming back to Berlin to get married. I was so surprised (practically shocked) that I wasn't capable of telling him to stay where he was.

When and where did you receive a proposal of marriage? Did you accept the proposal at the time? How did you feel-what was your reaction?

In a letter after he had gone back to the States. I was stunned and I guess excited.

What were the reactions of your parents, relatives and friends upon learning you were in love with an American military man and accepted his proposal of marriage?

My mother didn't like it too well. She didn't want me to leave. I was her sole support.

What were the official requirements for marriage? Do you feel obstacles were put in the way and if so, why? How long did it take before your were officially married?

As he was still a civilian when he came back to Berlin in December, 1950, there were no obstacles to get married.

Where were you married? Describe such things as the setting and those in attendance.

We were married on the 13th of December 1950 at the "Standesamt" in Zehlendorf with two of his American friends as witnesses and a few attendants. Had the reception at the Tempelhof Officers' Club.

If married in Germany what adjustments did you have to make to be with your husband? Where did you live, etc.?

Since he had to return to the States after a week, I still lived with my mother and kept on working at the Public Information Office. In the meantime I was waiting for my visa, and that is actually when the trouble started. I was put off with assorted kinds of lame excuses, that they were still investigating. After six months went by, I finally paid the American in Berlin a visit, and wouldn't you know, within a week I was in possession of the visa.

Where, when, and how did you go to the States?

I left Berlin June of 1951, flew to Amsterdam, and from there to New York and on to Dallas where he awaited me.

Did you speak English when you arrived? How were you treated and how were you helped to adjust to the new country? Did your husband's relatives and friends go out of their way to be of help and make you feel welcome?

I spoke English since I was ten years old, having lived in Montreal, Canada for nine years and attending schools there. So there was no problem in adjusting to the life in the USA. Nobody could tell that I was German until I told them—I had no accent whatsoever. We lived in Grand Prairie, Texas, in a garage apartment, and the only adjustment I had to make was to get used to the heat. I tried to beat it by submerging myself in a tub of cold water every few hours. None of his relatives lived near us but we did visit his sister and family in Oklahoma.

Describe how through the years your adjustment developed.

As the years went on and I became involved with the more active. The aggressive type of the American people made my gentle and polite upbringing disposition dwindle. I had to learn to assert myself, not getting pushed around.

Do you have children? If so give an indepth elaboration regarding their births, upbringing and present status.

We had four children – Three girls and one boy. The oldest, Beatrice was born on Okinawa. The other three in Mount Holly, New Jersey. Their upbringing depended solely on me (not monetary wise), since he was constantly on trips.

Beatrice earned a Bachelor, Master and Ph. D. Degree and is now Assist Vice President for Institutional Planning Research Policy Analysis at Southeastern Louisiana University.

Patty has her Bachelors Degree, works with an import export company (overseas department), and is leader of a Girl Scout Troop.

Duane received a Bachelor of Science and Master Degree; earned a full scholarship and fellowship and is a Phi Beta Kappa. He works for CompuServe in Columbus, Ohio, as a software engineer.

Marilyn has a BS degree and earned an MD degree, on an Air Force scholarship, from Louisiana State University School of Medicine in New Orleans.

Have you ever returned to Germany to visit your relatives? If so, were your husband and children with you? In turn have your relatives visited you in the States?

Returned to Germany several times to visit relatives and friends. Forrest and I visited three times, and Beatrice at age 16 accompanied me on a tour through Germany and other countries once. I traveled by myself once to visit a former school mate and a friend I worked with some years ago in Berlin. None of my relatives visited here, except my mother who came over here permanently, living alternately with my sister and me.

Why are you so proud and happy that the love of your life became your husband?

I don't quite know how to answer this question. Whether proud and happy, I don't know. Our road through 46 years was not always smooth and a bed of roses. Some men are difficult to live with and can't adjust to married life. At times I still ask myself and wonder what it would have been like, if I had stayed where I was.

PHOTO TAKEN 1983 FOR DIRECTORY OF PRESBYTERIAN CHURCH, SUMMERVILLE, SOUTH CAROLINA.

FAMILY OF FORREST AND HEDDA OTT – FROM YEARS PAST. BACK ROW: SON, DUANE, FORREST, AND DUANE'S WIFE, CHRISTINE. 2ND ROW: DAUGHTERS CAPT. MARILYN O. MORA, MD; PATRICIA O. WESSINGER; DR. BEATRICE O. BALDWIN, VC, PH.D.; AND HEDDA. FRONT ROW: MATTHEW BALDWIN, BEATRICE'S SON, AND MARILYN'S DAUGHTER, MICHELLE.

CHAPTER 7

*L*oves That Have Lasted

Deep love, character, developed by hardship and determination, plus willingness to place the well being of the other ahead of one's own self is the background that has led to such solid marriages. A separation is made here of the four grooms (Severino DiCocco, Paul Hawkins, William Michaels and James Spatafora) who were still in the military and had to overcome the strain placed upon all military personnel attempting to marry German civilians; and the fifth groom (Forrest Ott) who went back to Germany as a civilian and married with none of the obstacles placed before the aforementioned. All five marriages have endured the strains of time and developed a family tree that each can be proud of.

To facilitate readability, I will combine all four grooms, who because they were active members of the military were subject to its strict rules. References, of which they are unaware, such as a common thread that runs within them (including their brides), will refer to the many similarities they have to each other in the group. Rather than elaborating the similarities in a list type form, I will continue with additional information about these outstanding brides and grooms. If you haven't already done so by having read the previous chapters, see if you become aware of the similarities. The groom who returned to Berlin as a civilian to marry his German bride will be treated separately from the other.

PHOTO TAKEN IN APRIL, 1996—AND SEVERINO'S UNIFORM STILL FITS HIM.

Severino DiCocco was an active Berlin Airlift member of the military who helped provide the important recreation facilities at Rhein Main Air Base, for the American military personnel under the stressful pressure of the Airlift.

Years return in seconds to Severino when the movie "The Big Lift" appears on the TV screen, as all of the scenes in the movie involving the orderly room and barracks were shot in his squadron's orderly room (53rd Troop Carrier Squadron). The scene where the men arrived at the barracks showed what the airlift participants nicknamed "Rhein Mud" because when it rained there was mud throughout the air base. To reproduce the "Rhein Mud" the movie makers had the fire trucks put loads of water all over the place.

Whenever Montgomery Clift went to see his commander, it was Severino's squadron's orderly room.

At the time of this book's writing Severino has been continuing his involvement in researching the history of his church which celebrated its 1st Centennial on June 14, 1997. He has been going to the State Library to look at micro-films of the local area newspapers starting with 1895. It took about four hours just to view one year.

Severino does small repairs around their church complex. He is the president of the Church's Senior Group which is checking into what can be done to encourage seniors to remain in the area instead of moving South, etc.. They are looking at low-cost housing combined with various levels of medical help. Even looking at the possibility of the hospitals converting their excess bed space into health care (live-in) for seniors.

All of the above is done with inner ease and self-confidence because he has his wife **Anna Maria** at his side. In these days of short lived marriages **Severino DiCocco** the Groom and **Anna Maria (Bopp) DiCocco** the Bride have a lot to be proud of!!!

PHOTO OF PAUL
TAKEN IN 1951.

Paul Hawkins having been trained in maintenance of the AN/CP-5 medium range search radar for stationary targets that were modified and placed on the building at Tempelhof Airport for moving target indication. This was the first of its kind anywhere. Ground controlled approach (GCA) radar was important because it was used to locate the aircraft not only on course to the runway but also to keep it on the correct angle or glide path for proper touchdown. Radar played an extremely important role in the success of the Berlin Airlift.

As a Private First Class, Paul was not kept too informed as to how things came to be in the airlift. The powers that be, who planned the airlift knew that they had to have some way of keeping the aircraft in the twenty mile wide corridor and also to keep a certain separation between the aircraft. They were considering what type of radar to use. Paul doesn't know who decided on the AN/CPS-5 radar. It was designed for a medium range target search for early warning. It had the same problem as other radars the targets up close reflected back onto the scope as ground clutter. In Berlin, with all of its buildings, the center of the scope was almost all white with ground clutter.

In Mineola, New York, Airbourne Instruments Laboratory was working on a Moving Target Indicator system that could be combined with a modified AN/CPS-5 radar to eliminate the ground clutter problem. This system used a mercury delay line to delay one pulse long enough to allow it to be reversed and compared with the next incoming pulse. Thus, for stationary targets the reflection would be canceled out. This allows the operator to see the target all the way down to the ground, and even into the parking area. Anything that moved showed up sometimes even birds.

Another innovation was the video mapping machine. This machine used a scaled down negative of the area of Berlin as well as the Russian Airfield in the vicinity of Berlin. The video mapping was synchronized with the antenna so that on the radar scope the operator had lines to guide him in the movements of the aircraft.

General Tunner liked to go to the CPS-5 Maintenance Office where he was able to watch the movement of the aircraft on the monitor without disturbing the operations in the Operations Center.

When **Paul Hawkins** the Groom, finished his military service he became a Pastor and teacher. Eva became the perfect Pastor's wife to Paul. So ideal is their marriage that they are as much in love now as the day they were married. Nothing further need be said to illustrate this point than their own words extrapolated from the questionnaire. **Eva Hawkins** the Bride, comments, "He is the best husband and father any woman can wish for," and Paul's statement, "I feel like I cheated all the others who might have stolen her from me. We decided when we married that it would be for life. My only regret is that I have only one life with her. But we are going to make it as long as possible."

PHOTO OF BILL TAKEN IN CELLE, WEST GERMANY IN THE SPRING OF 1949.

William R. Michaels as a flight engineer in the Airlift had flown 174 missions into Berlin when he returned to the states August 8, 1949. Bill kept a diary of his experiences in the Airlift which he called "MEMORIES OF THE BERLIN AIRLIFT." Both his experiences and the manner in which it is written makes the reader feel they have gone back in time and are actually there participating with him.

Bill had many near misses and dangerous moments. One night while in line on the runway his pilot was told to hold his position as another plane was going to make a go-round at a specific altitude. Instead of going over them the plane was heading straight towards them. His pilot hit the throttle fast and got the plane off the runway. Had he not done so the oncoming plane would have crashed right into them.

Once shortly after takeoff for flight to Berlin an engine was lost and the remainder of the flight continued with three engines. The flight continued at an assigned altitude of 4500 feet in almost an unbroken layer of clouds. Upon breaking through the clouds while on a GCA (Ground Control Approach by radar), a British controller from Gatow shouted, "233, 233, overshoot! overshoot! overshoot!" Immediately below and slightly ahead was a Lancastrian tanker (British plane) that had lost its radio and was hedge-hopping to Berlin. It hadn't been seen on radar until it cleared the ridge Bill's plane was landing on. The planes came so close that Bill could see the pilot's red hair.

The Russian planes continually harassed but never fired upon Airlift planes. No pilot Bill ever flew with gave the harassment a second thought. This harassment appeared to end when the P-47 "airspeed check aircraft" was implemented. The P-47s, were armed with rockets and would suddenly appear below the left wing and fly for a short period of time and then peel-off to go to the Airlift plane behind.

On clear nights the Russians would sometimes attempt to ruin night vision by directing powerful searchlights at the Airlift planes. But soon pilots were prepared for it and placed maps and other large pieces of paper inside the windshield and side windows.

Once just before takeoff, two civilians were met by the pilot who obviously had expected them and they entered the plane. After a short distance, in the flight at a 4000 foot altitude while flying toward what appeared to be a Russian fighter base, the civilians had the pilot drop to a 1000 foot altitude so they could photograph the base. It could then be plainly seen what looked like fighter planes were actually only frames covered with burlap. Photos were taken by one of the civilian and the pilot returned the plane to the 4000 foot altitude.

As previously mentioned, Bill had a very difficult time in his attempt to get his first date with Annie for she insisted she would not date a married man and he "looked married." Were one to speak to Bill now knowing his Annie is up in Heaven they would almost feel the aura of his love for her that generates from his heart.

Because the following is so powerful I will quote **William R. Michaels'** words verbatim about his **Annie (Kirschbaum) Michaels** which is taken from his "A Love Story."

"It was the latter part of June 1949, I had just returned from Berlin, having completed my normal 12 hour duty shift as a flight engineer. Since I was not scheduled to fly until the next morning at 7AM. I decided to visit my fiancee who lived with her parents in Celle.

Arriving at the apartment, I found her distraught and crying, but very happy to see me. I asked her what was wrong. She told me that she had a horrible dream and was unable to get back to sleep afterward. She said that in her dream I was flying at night and my aircraft caught fire and crashed, killing the entire crew. To ease the situation a bit, I asked her if she could remember the large numbers on the tail of the plane. If she could not remember the numbers, I intended to stress the point that she merely had a bad a dream and that it was nothing to worry about.

"What do I know about Tail Numbers?" she answered, "I have never seen your airplane and you never talk about your job." I asked her to concentrate on what she saw in her dream and to try to remember any numbers. (Why I insisted on this point, I don't know.) She thought for a few minutes and said that she seemed to remember the numbers "236". Now it was my turn to get shook-up! My usual aircraft was "233" which had recently returned to the States for a 1000 hour inspection. The aircraft I had received to replace it was Tail Number "236."

Later that day my fiancée asked me not to fly for a short while. Since I had completed more that 150 flights to Berlin and really wanted a break, I requested to be relieved from regular flying duty and was officially relieved on 28 June 1949, and assigned to maintenance with no change in duty shift.

A short time later, around midnight, "236" had been loaded and was ready to go on the next block but the flight engineer who had replaced me could not be found. I offered to take the flight but the chief said that since I was no longer on the flying status I could not take it. While this discussion was going on, TSgt Herbert Heinig, my room-mate who had been on leave, came into the flight-line office and said that since he had slept all day and needed the flight time, he would take the flight.

During that block, "236" suffered an uncontrollable in-flight fire and, the crew was unable to leave the airplane. It crashed during a night landing attempt in a meadow in East Germany which resulted in the death of all three crew members.

The next morning I returned to my quarters to find my bedding and my footlocker gone and my wall locker open and empty. I hurried to the orderly room to find out what was going on. The adjutant looked up as I entered, his face turned white and he said, "My God, Sgt Michaels, you're dead!"

The assignment roster still showed me assigned to "236." I told the adjutant that Tsgt Heinig had been on the flight. This further complicated matters since Herbie had not signed in from leave.

For some time afterward, it was an eerie sensation to see the shocked or startled looks on the faces of people I knew who were seeing me for the first time since the accident."

Bill's love for **Annie** began the first time he saw her, and grew stronger and stronger as years went by. As he stated, "We had 37 wonderful, fulfilling years together before her death on the last day of 1986." **Annie's** love for **Bill** grew just as strong!

Her clairvoyant dream saved **Bill** from the fatal plane crash during the Airlift. Though now in Heaven, **Annie** is in **Bill's** heart every minute of the day and no doubt still remains his **"Guardian Angel."**

PHOTO TAKEN IN JUNE, 1988. FIRST TIME JAMES (NOW A LT. COL.) AND COL. GAIL HALVORSEN, THE "BERLIN CANDY BOMBER," MET EACH OTHER AGAIN IN BERLIN IN 39 YEARS.

James Spatafora – Accidents, injuries and deaths were bound to occur in such an enormous undertaking as the Berlin Airlift. James who arrived at Rhein Main Air Base as a P-51 hydraulic specialist was immediately made the one and only C-54 hydraulic specialist at the base. He had never seen the C-54 hydraulic system before and had to learn it on his own for there was no one there to teach him.

One day in October of 1949 just after he had changed the nose wheel and tire assembly on a C-54 loaded with coal and gasoline fuel, it was lined up on the taxiway headed toward the runway. About an hour earlier a brushfire had started at the end of the runway with smoke obscuring the takeoff end of the runway. The Base Fire Department responded and put out the fire. In those days very little of Rhein Main Air Base was paved. The runway, parts of the taxiway and a few of the streets near the headquarters were paved but the rest of the base was "mud" either liquid in summer or frozen mud in the winter. The fire truck was traveling West toward the sunset as that day aircraft were taxiing toward the East to the takeoff end of the runway.

James had just run across the taxiway to get to the mobile snack bar to get coffee and a donut, and saw the fire truck (blinded by the sunset and landing lights on the leading aircraft) headed toward the #2 propeller on the first aircraft. At the last moment the fire truck swerved to the right and went through the propeller arc of #1 propeller. The pilot shut the engines down but it was too late, the fire truck's engine compartment went through the driver's compartment, killed the GI fireman driver, then threw the German fireman who had been sitting next to the driver out. As the truck passed through the propeller and under the wing, the wing broke off the two fire fighting foam turret nozzles which now looked like two "snake fangs" upside down. The jagged foam nozzles ripped the bottom off the wing of the lead aircraft and the truck continued driverless down the taxiway. Although the truck had slowed down a bit it was still going fast enough to get to the left wing of the aircraft and tear two grooves in the bottom of the wing and finally stopped when it hit the left main gear of the aircraft.

High octane gasoline poured out of the gashes in the wing all over the "stalled" truck engine which was still running until it hit the left main gear. The gasoline went all over the hot engine, the ignition system and headlights were still "on." It was a miracle nothing made an electrical spark to set the whole ramp on fire. James and others rushed to the driver but there was nothing they could do for him.

They then went to the aircraft with hand operated fire extinguishers but would have been helpless if a fire did start so they stood guard at the aircraft all night until the next day to keep people away until all the gasoline had drained from the aircraft and had completely evaporated and the battery went totally "dead" on the fire truck. When it was finally "safe" they lifted the aircraft and pulled out the fire truck.

James will gladly show you the Bos'n "Pipe" he wears to this day in honor of the role the US Navy played in the Berlin Airlift. Not only did the Navy fly its R5-D planes in the Airlift, the fact that its R5-D and the C-54 of the Air Force were manufactured by Douglas Aircraft made the parts for these planes interchangeable. The Navy was both generous and cooperative in giving aircraft parts it had available at the Air Base which might have taken James and others sometime to get through channels. Such was the case in the repair of the aircraft mentioned above.

James and Ellie have been involved in and with many fine and worthy causes and organizations. With James there is the "Toastmasters International," fund raisers for orphanages, thrift shops, raffles, fashion shows to raise funds for worthy causes, church activities; breakfasts, dinners, and many other activities. Ellie has been involved in Air Force Base "thrift shops" on many Air Bases in the US and overseas for at least forty years.

James belongs to three national model railroad clubs: the Train Collectors Association (TCA), the Lionel Collectors Club of America (LCCA), the Train Collectors Train Operating Society (TTOS) as well as a "computer" users group. Both James and Ellie are members of the Berlin Airlift Veterans Association (at this time James is the organization's Air Force Representative) and the Berlin Airlift Historical Foundation (with the gratitude to Tim Chopp, BAHF's president, James is a volunteer crew member). (Author's note: most if not all Brides and Grooms "Stars" in this book are members of both organizations.)

James rose in rank from a Private in the United States Army Air Corps to Lieutenant Colonel in the United States Air Force. He said **Ellie** helped him all along the way through, in addition to raising their three children almost all by herself.

MARCH 6, 1998, FORREST AS AN OFFICIAL GREETER OF THE C 17 "THE SPIRIT OF BERLIN" AT ITS ARRIVAL AT THE US AIR FORCE BASE AT CHARLESTON, SOUTH CAROLINA BEFORE LEAVING FOR BERLIN, GERMANY TO PARTICIPATE IN THE 50TH BERLIN AIRLIFT ANNIVERSARY CELEBRATIONS.

Forrest E. Ott was a member of the 1946th Army Airways Communications System Squadron (AACS) at Tempelhof Army Air Base during the Berlin Airlift. He had been an Air Traffic Controller at the Frankfurt Air Traffic Control Center prior to the blockade of Berlin by the Soviet Union. Forrest was transferred from the Frankfurt Air Traffic Control Center to the Berlin Air Traffic Control (which was called the Berlin Air Safety Center) early in April, 1948. He had his baggage, car (a little 500 cc Fiat Topolino), and dog loaded aboard a Frankfurt AACS Squadron C-47 and flown to Berlin. The commander did not want Forrest to take the chance of having any "problems" at the checkpoints by driving to Berlin.

At the time, all Air Traffic Controllers in Europe were Officer's and Pilots. Once the Airlift started, these pilots could not get local flights in order to maintain their proficiency and receive their monthly flying pay. The only way for them to fly was on airlift aircraft. So, they worked 12 hour shifts as controllers. They would work three day shifts, and then three night shifts. This way they would have two days for flying. Forrest flew as an aircraft commander on C-47's until the C-54's arrived. He had never flown a 4-engine aircraft and made up his mind that he wanted to become a C-54 aircraft commander.

The way he worked it: as he was nearing the end of a series of work shifts, he would inquire of inbound C-54's which one had an Instructor Pilot aboard. When he found one, he would ask to ride out to their home station with them. They always said "yes." While in flight he would ask the co-pilot if he would like to take a rest. Again, they always said "yes." Then, most of the time the Instructor would offer him the left (Pilot's) seat which is what Forrest wanted.

When they arrived at the home base of the crew (usually Fassberg or Rhein Main) he would ask to be placed on a crew for the next two missions. Forrest would fly those two missions as a Co-pilot and then deadhead back to Berlin (with an Instructor). If he was lucky enough to be paired with an Instructor for the two missions, he would get at least two or probably more opportunities in the left seat. So, in about 24 hours, he would have logged three aircraft missions and received a lot of good training. He was checked out as an Aircraft Commander on C-54's in July 1949 and flew several of his last missions as an Aircraft Commander. He had been successful and his last goal in flying at the time had been accomplished.

Air Traffic Controllers problems always existed but the biggest problems usually occurred during the winter months with bad weather. Forrest became a "Senior Fog and Smogger" which meant that he had more than five landings with the ceiling less than 200 feet, and/or visibility of less than one-half mile. In January of 1949, area radar was installed at Tempelhof which simplified traffic control immensely. This, Ground Control Approach (GCA) radar was a major factor leading to the success of the Berlin Airlift.

Forrest retired from the US Air Force on October 31, 1971, as a Lt. Col. with some 18,928 hours of flight time. Because of his outstanding background which included participation in the Berlin Airlift he was asked to be a member of the committee to greet the arrival of the C-17 Globemaster III at Charleston Air Force Base in South Carolina. This C-17 and had been flown directly from its manufacturer to Charleston. From its stop-over at Charleston it was flown to Berlin, Germany where on May 13, 1998 it was officially christened "Spirit of Berlin" and played a major role in the 50th Berlin Airlift anniversary ceremony celebration held at Tempelhof Airport.

Forrest has received a vast amount of news coverage relating to legendary accomplishments in the cockpit of various aircraft, amassing more than 25,000 flying hours. This 25,000 flying hour feat was reached on March 7, 1998 when he flew this record flight with two Citadel cadets who were receiving an orientation flight with the Charleston Civil Air Patrol. Upon landing he was greeted as a hero (and legend) by the awaiting party, receiving a plaque for his accomplishment.

Forrest Ott was awarded "The Order of the Palmetto," for years of Exemplary Service and Devotion to his Community, People and State. (This is the "highest" civilian award given by the State of South Carolina.)

Credit is due The Summerville Journal Scene, a newspaper in Charleston, South Carolina and the Airlift Dispatch, a newspaper of the USAF Charleston Base, for their cooperation in providing information pertaining to Lt. Col. Forrest E. Ott.

Though **Forrest** and his loving wife **Hedda** have been married for more than forty years and are proud of their four children and five grandchildren-one can't help wonder if **Hedda** ever adjusted to all the time **Forrest** spent with his other love . . . . **FLYING!**

CKNOWLEDGEMENTS

Appreciation of the following for information, and/or inspiration that helped make "BERLIN AIRLIFT: BRIDES & GROOMS CREATED" possible.

THE BERLIN CANDY BOMBER - The book written by world renowned Col. Gail Halvorsen, the "Berlin Candy Bomber"—a Berlin Airlift pilot who dropped parachutes laden with candy and gum for the children in blockaded Berlin. (Col. Halvorsen is one of the most sincerest persons this author knows.)

BLOCKADE AND AIRLIFT: LEGEND OR LESSON? - Editors: "Heinz-Gerd Reese, Michael Schroder and Manfred Schwarzkopf." "Heinz-Gerd Reese" is the Director of the "Berlin Airlift Gratitude Foundation" in Berlin, Germany.

OUTPOST BERLIN: THE HISTORY OF THE AMERICAN MILITARY FORCES IN BERLIN, 1945-1994 - "Henrik Bering" has obviously done a "tremendous" amount of research to have obtained such indepth facts of the time.

SODAT - "Siegfried Knappe" a German soldier tells how his rapid rise in ranks put him in position where he could have killed Hitler. He didn't do so as he felt that would have made Hitler a martyr. Mr. Knappe also notes most members of the German Army were just soldiers of their country not Nazi's.

THE BERLIN AIRLIFT - An outstanding audio-visual documentary produced and directed by "Robert E. Frye."

BERLIN AIRLIFT VETERANS ASSOCIATION (BAVA) - Composed of Berlin Airlift Veterans (and friends). Many didn't know the importance of what they were doing at the time but now know, are proud and "highly" appreciated for having done it. The author wonders if this book would have been written had he not met, been made an honorary-life member of the BAVA (1992), and received such tremendous cooperation in the process of research.

BAVA WEB SITE -
HTTP://WWW.KONNECTIONS.COM/AIRLIFT/INDEX.HTML
WEB MASTER: "Mark Vaughn" - GANDOLF@KONNECTIONS.COM

BERLIN AIRLIFT HISTORICAL FOUNDATION (BAHF) - Found, purchased and made a C-54 plane (type used in the Berlin Airlift) airworthy and into a flying museum and classroom of the Berlin Airlift era. The plane has been named, the "Spirit of Freedom" and is filled with simulated sacks of coal, flour and other memorabilia. In May, 1998 this author was a guest aboard the "Spirit of Freedom's" historic flight that departed from Brooklyn, New York; with landings at Massachusetts, Canada, Iceland, Scotland, England and Berlin, Germany to be part of the first major Berlin Airlift 50th Anniversary ceremony celebrations at Tempelhof Airport. The author was happily impressed at the "tremendous" outpouring of enthusiasm the "Spirit of Freedom" always received.

GERMAN CONSULATE GENERAL - "Werner Schmitz" former Consul of Protocol, New York City, New York

GERMAN INFORMATION CENTER - New York City, New York

CHECKPOINT CHARLIE MUSEUM - Rainer Hildebrandt, Director, Berlin, Germany

INDIVIDUALS AND ORGANIZATIONS - too numerous to mention - the following are but a few:
    Col. Kenneth Herman (Ret.), President of the BAVA;
    Fred Hall, member of both BAVA and BAHF;
    John Macia, Director of Publicity and Public Relations, BAVA;
    Tim Chopp, President and Board Chairman of BAHF;
    Johanna Hoppe, Berlin, Germany
    Mark White, former Director of Radio and Television, United States Armed Forces Network, Berlin, Germany. Mark remained in Berlin.